The Art of War for Women

CURRENCY   DOUBLEDAY

NEW YORK   LONDON   TORONTO

SYDNEY   AUCKLAND

The Art
of War
for Women

SUN TZU'S ANCIENT STRATEGIES

AND WISDOM FOR WINNING AT WORK

CHIN-NING CHU

A CURRENCY BOOK
PUBLISHED BY DOUBLEDAY

Published in the United States by Doubleday, an imprint of
The Doubleday Broadway Publishing Group, a division of
Random House, Inc., New York.
www.currencybooks.com

CURRENCY is a trademark of Random House, Inc., and
DOUBLEDAY is a registered trademark of Random House, Inc.

Book design by Gretchen Achilles
Calligraphy by

廖繼敏
LIAO CHI MIN

Library of Congress Cataloging-in-Publication Data
Chu, Chin-Ning.
The art of war for women / Chin-Ning Chu.
p.   cm.
"A Currency book."
(hardcover : alk. paper)
1. Success—Psychological aspects. 2. Success in business.
3. Self-preservation. 4. Military art and science. I. Title.
BF637.S8C4777   2007
158—dc22
2006038567

ISBN: 978-0-385-51840-6

PRINTED IN THE UNITED STATES OF AMERICA

SPECIAL SALES Currency Books are available at special discounts
for bulk purchases for sales promotions or premiums. Special editions,
including personalized covers, excerpts of existing books, and corporate
imprints, can be created in large quantities for special needs.
For more information, write to Special Markets, Currency Books,
specialmarkets@randomhouse.com.

1   3   5   7   9   10   8   6   4   2

FIRST EDITION

CONTENTS

outsmart the competition or "simply" working to gain a promotion at work.

No matter what your goal is, Master Sun's principles remain the same and so do his strategies: His advice is always designed to produce the best result with the least amount of conflict.

That's why *Sun Tzu's Art of War* is particularly appropriate for women. Let's face it: As intelligent and accomplished as we may be, there are very few of us who are comfortable with either direct confrontation or situations where our triumph means someone else's defeat. We are natural negotiators and problem solvers; most of us prefer win-win situations to winner-takes-all.

But there is another reason *The Art of War* is particularly appropriate for us. Although Sun Tzu's book is about the application of strategies, every one of those strategies begins with having a deep understanding of the people we will be dealing with and our environment. But most important, it also requires us to understand ourselves—our strengths and weaknesses, our goals and fears. In other words, this book is not about applying a series of rules coldly and dispassionately, but rather about integrating ourselves into the strategies we will employ. It is about building naturally on who we are and embracing our own unique personalities and talents to achieve what we want. Just as Master Sun recognized that you cannot separate what you do from who you are, this book will teach you how to use what you have to get what you want.

Unless you are willing to examine your personal, philosophical, and emotional issues, you cannot fully comprehend the application of Sun Tzu's ideas. He makes no division between the tangible and abstract or the emotional and the rational. This book will teach you to assess your liabilities and devise strategies to turn them into strengths. Similarly, you will explore how your greatest strengths can become your biggest weaknesses.

This is not a feel-good book. (But I am confident you will feel good after reading it.) It is not a motivational book. (But I promise you will

It's About the Art, Not the War

In the West, when we think of war, we imagine opposing generals turning loose troops to conquer one another. At the end of the battle, the winning side is the one with the greatest number of soldiers still standing. So, not surprisingly, when we hear about a book called *The Art of War for Women* we think of battle, casualties, brutality.

But Sun Tzu (Sun is his last name, Tzu means Mr.), the man who wrote *The Art of War* some 2,500 years ago, was Chinese, and the Chinese think of war differently than we do in the West. To them, war does not revolve around fighting. It is about determining the most efficient way of gaining victory with the *least* amount of conflict.

This distinction between the eastern and western philosophies of warfare is important to keep in mind. Indeed, it goes to the very heart of my book. *Sun Tzu's Art of War*, which has been studied by military leaders, politicians, and businessmen around the world for hundreds of years, is not about war at all. It is a set of strategic thinking skills designed to help you achieve your objective in the most efficient way possible.

That objective can be a military victory, but it can also be winning on the business battlefield—whether you are trying to *be motivated to achieve what you want, once you are done.) Ultimately, its purpose is to provide women with the strategies we all need to overcome the obstacles that stand in the way of our achieving everything we want.*

In the pages ahead, you will learn how to:

- Win without confrontation.

- Fully integrate your ethics into the practical demands of earning a living. (You *can* succeed without compromising your integrity.)

- Develop the crucial ability to see the "big picture" and master strategic thinking in its entirety.

- Become more innovative, adaptive, and creative by integrating your own style and philosophy into every action you take.

And perhaps most important, you will learn to:

- Translate the universally applicable strategies of *Sun Tzu's Art of War* into tools you can use to succeed in whatever you do.

By mastering Sun Tzu's strategies, you will see what other people are blind to and hear the silent messages that they cannot.

This Book Is Written for You

You can become a master strategist, whether you set your sights on being a CEO, entrepreneur, schoolteacher, stockbroker, movie producer, or astronaut. Even if your aim in life is to be a good mother and a happier person (and these are noble aims indeed), studying of *The Art of War for Women* will help you transform your disadvantages into advantages.

Whether you're more comfortable in glass slippers or combat boots, you can learn how to think like an effective strategist and warrior.

All things are possible when you master *Sun Tzu's Art of War*.

A Holistic Approach to Winning

One final note, before we start.

While this book will empower women, it is not antimen. I love men. I am indebted to many men who, throughout my career, have given me the lift that I needed simply because they genuinely wanted me to succeed. But we cannot ignore the fact that women have unique talents that, if embraced, will help us level the corporate playing field. We no longer have to do things the way men have done them—we can do things *our* way.

Men have taken to the concepts of war and battle like fish to water. For thousands of years men have fought life's battles. From the battlefield to the corner office, they have been trained to think like warriors.

That *may* be fine for them. But that approach is not always right for us.

My goal here is to examine strategies that can help every woman celebrate her femininity to the fullest, while gaining the freedom to soar to personal and professional heights.

The Art of War is about life, death, fear, courage, subterfuge, integrity, victory and defeat, honor and disgrace, profit and loss, unpredictability and simplicity, accountability and responsibility.

It is also about relationships and interacting with those you view as generals, your fellow soldiers—even your competitors.

Most of all, it is about how you deal with the cards that life has dealt you—it is a holistic approach to winning.

Introduction
Sun Tzu and His Art of War

Befor, I wanted to marry a millionaire. Now I want to become one."

So read the billboard for a career placement agency that caught my eye recently.

What struck me is how universal this sentiment has become—it is not just American women who want to become successful in business. You find the same attitude among women in Canada, Germany, France, China, and England. It is an international phenomenon, a bond of womanhood that cuts across and beyond cultures and national boundaries.

For most of the twentieth century, people thought it was impossible for a woman to achieve everything she wanted; women were told that our attempts to "have it all" were causing us to become physically and mentally frustrated and overwhelmed.

That was nonsense.

In order to compete in a male-dominated world, we women have always had to be twice as good at our jobs—while taking home a fraction of the pay.

Regardless of how much men *think* they know women, only a woman knows how difficult it is to be a woman. British economist Herbert Spencer could have been referring to the silent strength of women when he coined the phrase "survival of the fittest." But now that we have survived thousands of years of second-class citizenship, it's time for us to thrive—in business and in our lives. And this book can help us do that.

Ancient (but Eternal) Truths

Sun Tzu's wisdom may be ancient, but it is eternal. *The Art of War* draws from Taoist philosophy, which is based on observing the rules that exist in nature. By studying nature for more than five thousand years, Taoist philosophers have created a series of principles that they believe govern every living thing, including humans.

Since Master Sun based his book on universal principles, it is not surprising that it can be applied to every aspect of our lives, including our careers. In fact, I am surprised that no one—until now—has written a book that teaches women how to apply the strategies in *The Art of War* to their careers and lives.

After all, Sun Tzu believed that the best strategy is to win without fighting. Now, what in that wouldn't appeal to every woman?

The strategies that you will read about in these pages are a perfect match for women's greatest natural strengths. For thousands of years, women living in male-dominated societies have learned the value of appearing more submissive than we really are. We have learned to allow men to think they are in charge and how to get our way by pretending to go along with them.

Intuitively, women have always used some of the Chinese art of war strategies when negotiating with our husbands, lovers, children, bosses, friends, customers, and clients. We just didn't know we were actually strategists in disguise. It is about time that we build on our natural abilities and learn how to use the full spectrum of the strategies and tactics that are contained in *Sun Tzu's Art of War*.

Why this particular book? Because among all the ancient strategy treatises—and many were written in ancient China—*Sun Tzu's Art of War*, written before 512 B.C., is currently the most popular in business—and for good reason. It is infinitely adaptable to today's work environment.

Because the lessons are so powerful, let's take a step back and see where this wisdom comes from.

Meet Sun Tzu

Where there is power, you will likely find Sun Tzu—on Wall Street, on Capitol Hill, on bookshelves in the poshest corner offices. During congressional hearings, staffers—and even the occasional congressman or senator—pull out their paperback editions of *The Art of War* and flip through the pages wondering "Which strategy should I use now?"

But while almost every statement in the book seems relevant, few readers seem able to find the specific strategy that will turn the tide in their favor. Invariably, they end up frustrated.

It is a common reaction.

One Sunday morning I received a phone call from Japan. A U.S. Marine colonel stationed there had telephoned to tell me how much he enjoyed studying *Thick Face, Black Heart*, one of my previous books. As one topic led to another, he began speaking more candidly with me, opening up.

Finally he confided, "As a Marine officer, it is part of my

training that I study Sun Tzu. To tell you the truth, I have read *Sun Tzu's Art of War* many times but I still do not really understand it."

This is the most frequent complaint I have heard from clients, friends, and readers. They tell me they have not really been able to assimilate, understand, and apply *Sun Tzu's Art of War*, even after many readings. This is not due to a lack of intellect, but rather because Master Sun didn't write *The Art of War* to create a bestseller. He wrote it because he was looking for a job.

How Sun Tzu's Art of War *Came to Be*

Sun Tzu was not a military man when he wrote his art of war treatise. A farmer by profession and a self-taught philosopher, Master Sun descended from a Chinese scholar-military family.

Because his grandfather was a military general, Sun enjoyed the unique advantage of having full access to rare military books.

This is no small point. In the days before both paper and the printing press, each copy of a book needed to be created by hand on bamboo or wood strips. As a result, there were very few books in circulation, and military books—given their specialized nature—were even rarer. It was not uncommon for those who possessed a copy of an art of war book—as all books about military strategy were known—to safeguard the almost sacred object with their lives.

You can clearly see Sun's background reflected in *The Art of War*. His strategies draw both from previously successful military campaigns and an understanding of nature, something that comes naturally to a farmer.

He spent a lot of time looking for extraordinary strategies in the ordinary world around him. He noticed, for example, how water will change its course when confronted with an obstacle

and yet still will have the ability—over time—to erode everything in its path. Or how the most deeply rooted tree will crack, in the face of strong winds, while a seemingly fragile blade of grass will simply bend—and survive.

In addition to his agrarian background and the exposure to military strategy, there is another factor that makes Sun Tzu unique.

Around 532 B.C., Sun, then in his late teens, escaped to Wu (south of today's Shanghai) after his father—a warrior himself—rebelled against the ruling royalty. Sun Tzu hid out for twenty years. During those two decades, he experienced firsthand the suffering and daily experiences of the common people and the underprivileged. He understood the pain of real life.

Sun Tzu had no distinguished teacher, nor did he hail from a highly distinguished or royal family. His wisdom emerged from his keen power of observation, his personal studies, the challenges he faced, and his contemplation of the unfolding of nature and the world around him.

As a young man, he wrote his *Bing Fa* (*bing* means soldier, *fa* means skill; the combination has been translated throughout the centuries as *The Art of War*) as a résumé, in the hopes of getting a job as the King of Wu's military commander.

Even given his humble background, his goal isn't as strange as it first sounds. Sun Tzu lived in the midst of the 550 years of China's civil war. Anyone who could provide to the kings and feudal lords strategies that would insure domination over their rivals would be guaranteed employment, regardless of their humble circumstances. Anyone who could present strategies that would help a king achieve his aim would leap from commoner to superstar overnight.

Tempted by the promise of fame, wealth, and glory, over two thousand military strategy books were written, Sun Tzu's among them.

The King of Wu, intrigued by *Sun Tzu's Art of War*, hired him as his military commander and put his strategy to the test. During one battle, with an army of only 20,000 men, Master Sun defeated the Kingdom of Zhou, which had a contingent of 200,000 men.

In 1772 *Sun Tzu's Art of War* was translated into French. It is widely believed that Napoléon read and adopted many of Master Sun's strategies. During Operation Desert Storm (the first Iraq war in 1990–91), as well as the Iraq war that began in 2003, officers in the U.S. Marine Corps were issued copies of *The Art of War* as standard battle gear.

Sun Tzu Wanted The Art of War *to Be Difficult*

The difficulty that the Marine colonel—and many others—have in understanding what Sun Tzu was trying to say has very little to do with the reader and very much to do with the author himself.

For one thing, Sun never intended the book to have a wide audience. From the language, form, and construction of his writing, I believe he was—in large part—writing the book not only for his employer, but also for himself, worrying more about his insights than his prose.

Writers understand well why someone might take this approach. You gain a deeper, more profound understanding of a specific subject by writing it down. Capturing your observations on paper allows you to easily revisit the thought and delve deeper into its meaning.

The fact that Sun Tzu wrote in such a cryptic, abstract fashion supports the argument that he intended his work to be read only by himself—and his employer. History tells us that the King of Wu didn't completely grasp the essence of the book because Sun was turned down seven times before the king agreed to see him. Furthermore, during his job interview, he asked Sun Tzu to demonstrate his art of war. Also, if the king had understood the power of Sun Tzu's book the first time he read it, he would not have repeatedly refused to employ Sun despite strong recommendations from his foreign minister.

But I believe there is a second reason the original text is so difficult to understand. To safeguard his knowledge, Master Sun deliberately made it obscure, so that the king would be forced to rely on him for interpretation, once he was hired.

This tactic had three benefits. First, it ensured that Sun Tzu would remain employed. The king could not simply read *The Art of War,* implement the strategy, and fire Sun (or execute him, as was so common in those days). He needed the author around to explain exactly what the text meant and how to best implement it.

Second, by making the text difficult to parse, Sun Tzu did not have to be overly concerned about losing his secrets, in the event the enemy got hold of his manuscript. (One of the reasons Gen. George S. Patton was able to defeat German general Erwin Rommel in Africa during World War II is that Patton had studied Rommel's book on warfare and knew the moves Rommel was likely to make in certain situations.)

Third, by keeping the knowledge obscure, Sun Tzu could protect himself against threats from others in his *own* army. His decision not to make all his knowledge immediately accessible calls to mind the kung fu master who never teaches his final, deadliest move to his students. If he taught them everything he knew, they could use those moves one day to eliminate him. His indiscretion could mean his death.

If Sun Tzu had wanted to open a school to teach or pass down his wisdom for posterity, as Confucius did, he would have provided examples as to exactly how he intended these strategies to be used. Master Sun made himself mysterious and indispensable by providing no examples, no anecdotes, nor sufficient historical references to show how he intended his knowledge to be employed.

Thus, the search to understand Sun Tzu has continued evolving, keeping westerners and Chinese alike intrigued for more than 2,500 years.

Scholars have delved deep into Chinese history to divine exactly how to apply Sun Tzu's theory, and each, it seems, has their own take. There are more than two hundred English versions of *Sun Tzu's Art of War* that are more or less translations and adaptations, while Chinese scholars have created thousands of versions with commentaries, examples, and interpretations for more than two millennia, trying to solve Sun's riddle. And yet in all that time there has never been a version of his work written strictly for women—until now.

Throughout the book I have included my translations of excerpts of *The Art of War*, which you'll recognize by the different typeface. Additionally, you will find boxes that include my own observations about Sun Tzu's philosophy. I have also provided space to allow you to reflect on how to adopt these strategies as your own. This book will not only instruct but also reflect like a mirror, revealing where you are, where you are going, and what you have to do to get there. It will also serve as a blueprint for your own one-of-a-kind résumé.

CHAPTER 1

Ji (Planning)
The Elements of Strategy

Before waging a war, the five elements that govern success must be examined. Only then can a proper assessment be done.

Those five elements are: 1. Tao (moral standing or ethics); 2. Tien (timing); 3. Di (terrain or resources); 4. Jiang (leadership); 5. Fa (managing).

The first chapter of *Sun Tzu's Art of War* contains the core message of the book and includes all the principles that will be discussed in the remaining twelve chapters.

Sun Tzu begins this chapter with a discussion of a concept called *Ji*.* Ji has a broad range of meanings: plotting and plan-

*To be completely accurate, some translations insert the word *shi*, which means "to start" or "begin," before the word *ji*. The original text used only the word *ji*.

ning, predicting, comparing, and analyzing. All these elements are part of "prewar" strategy—in other words, they're the steps you must take before you take any action.

Once you can understand these planning stages of life, the rest of Master Sun's strategies will become second nature. For this reason, I examine his first chapter in depth. According to Sun, five elements govern success and must be understood in the planning stages of any action.

TAO: Your moral standing and the motivation that drives your actions. If your moral position is pure, colleagues will be willing to go to the mat for your cause.

TIEN: Timing. There are certain times when you should take action, other times when it is far better to wait. *Tien* lets you know which way to decide.

DI: "Earth," "terrain," or "resources." *Di* refers to the obstacles that you face on your journey to success. Are you traveling over level ground? In other words, is everything going smoothly at work—or is each task akin to scaling a great mountain? *Di* also includes the distances you need to travel to accomplish your goal.

JIANG: "Leadership." Sun Tzu believed that a leader must be wise, trustful, benevolent, courageous, and strict.

FA: "Method" or "how to"—what we today would call managing. Your "army" must be well organized, disciplined, and responsible, and as a leader you must be strong, and merciless in your attempts to maintain order. (Notice that Master Sun has adopted the paradoxical elements of Tao and Fa as part of his strategic thinking. I will explain how you can master the balance between the two.)

Things to Keep in Mind When Adopting Strategy

Those who carefully calculate their strategies will be led to victory. Those who carelessly calculate their strategies will be led to defeat.

1. *None of the strategies in* Sun Tzu's Art of War *stands on its own.* All the elements are interrelated. In other words, strategy is not one-dimensional; it is multidimensional.

But unfortunately, books can only deliver one point at a time. As you read, you will see how the various pieces fit together. Don't worry, I will help.

2. *Play with the power of paradox.* Taoist philosophy, which *Sun Tzu's Art of War* is based on, recognizes that good and evil are not opposing forces. The opposites are not absolute; rather, they are related—just as we know beauty because we have also seen ugliness and know short only as it compares to tall. In Taoism, in *The Art of War,* there is no right and wrong, no black and white. Every action has its time and place, and the same action will lead to different results when your opponent or other circumstances are different. Confused? Good. This is the first step to understanding *The Art of War;* you have to give up your attachment to clear-cut realities and instead embrace the whole spectrum of colors of paradox and ambiguity. This is the foundation of the art of war and the art of life.

3. *Don't look for rules or consistency. The only rule is, there are no rules.* The stories that I use to bring *The Art of War* to life are provided to increase your understanding; they are not a formula to be followed. The specific subtleties of your situation—you, your opponent, your environment, your timing—will not be exactly the same as someone else's; therefore, the outcome cannot

be the same. When just one element is changed, the entire picture is altered.

As Sun Tzu wrote: "The strategy that provided you victory, may not be repeated in the same way."

4. *Strategy is not about overexercising your brain.* It is about understanding your place in the world around you. Think about water flowing downstream into a lake or ocean. There is a destination, but the course will change depending on the terrain. Strategy is not about rules; it's about adaptation.

With this by way of background, let's delve into the five elements—Tao, Tien, Di, Jiang, and Fa—in greater detail.

1.1
Tao (Righteousness)
How to Make Winning Decisions

Armed with the sense of righteousness and the blessings from Heaven, your army becomes fearless. Thus, they are willing to live and die for the purpose of realizing victory.

Of all the five strategies that make up *Sun Tzu's Art of War*, Tao is the most important. It is not by accident that Master Sun placed Tao first in his classic book on strategy.

Tao translates to "the way, rightness or morality," but that is only the beginning. Tao is defined as the force behind all creation. As the foremost Taoist philosopher, Lao Tzu, said when describing what we in the West would call God, "I do not know what to call Her, I call Her 'Tao.' "

(Note: In ancient Chinese writings all pronouns are implied. So I took the liberty of using the feminine form when it is appropriate.)

All things good, brilliant, righteous, creative, innovative, ecstatic, sweet, and joyful are rooted in Tao—the righteous way.

How Do I Make the Right Decisions?

The question you probably have by now is: How do I use Tao to help me succeed at work? It can be tempting to put short-term gains at our jobs ahead of doing what is righteous, but that is always a mistake. And it will almost always backfire painfully.

When one works against Tao, an ill fate awaits. As the great Chinese philosopher Mung Tzu said, "Tao always sides with the righteous." The more Tao we possess, the happier we are, and the more success we enjoy.

The list that follows can help you in making the right decisions.

The Tao of Decision Making

1. *Ask yourself: "How righteous is my objective?"* Every action you take can be measured on a scale of right to wrong. Before making any decision, you must ask what is motivating you.

For example, you may covet a promotion. But simply desiring a fancy title or a corner office is not consistent or inconsistent with Tao. It is simply a desire.

Make sure you know *why* you want the promotion. Is it for the additional pay? More recognition? To thumb your nose at the colleague you have been competing with?

All those things can be motivating forces; it is even possible that they can provide the drive that can help you move up the corporate ladder. But unless you enjoy doing the work associated with the new position, you are ensuring your defeat.

For example, in many companies, the title of sales manager is a more prestigious one than that of salesperson. However, if you hate managing people, don't like doing paperwork, and would much rather interact with clients, then a promotion is simply a prescription for disaster.

> If you don't have a righteous objective, eventually you will suffer. When you do the right thing for the right reason, the right result awaits.

Here's an example of righteousness. When Joann* left a Fortune 100 company to join a start-up, she left a $1 million retirement package behind. But as she told me, "It was the right thing to do. I traded a million dollars for a dream."

That dream initially required her to work longer hours for substantially less money, fewer perks, and no stock options. And in contrast with the security her former employer offered, there was no guarantee that the new company would succeed long term.

The new firm is now considered one of the best-managed, fastest-growing companies in the world—and thanks to stock options, awarded to Joann shortly after she joined the firm in recognition of the superior job she had done, she is now worth more than $10 million.

In today's fast-moving business world, you are never going to have enough data to make a "solid" decision, one that is ab-

---

*Throughout the book I am going to use fictitious names and camouflage a few of the telling details in the examples I present to protect the privacy of those involved. "Joann" doesn't really need such protection, but other women I mention will. The examples themselves are real.

solutely guaranteed to turn out to be the right choice. When in doubt, I ask a simple question: "Is this the righteous thing to do?"

Tao always leads you to victory, although sometimes the right result may take a while to appear.

2. The second question you must ask yourself before making any decision is: *Is this driven by my ego?* A supersized ego holds the seeds of self-destruction.

Heir to her family's banking fortune, Alice took over the CEO spot in the business when she was in her late thirties. She was, in short, a disaster. Convinced that she knew better, she refused to listen to opinions of her senior staff that were contrary to her own.

"I grew up in this business" was her standard answer when someone questioned her decisions.

Even worse, she seemed to care more about the perks that came with her office—which included a full-time chauffeur and cook—than she did the business herself. "Make sure they know who I am" was what she told her assistant every time she went out on an errand.

It perhaps wasn't surprising that she ran the business into the ground. Her bank was acquired by a far larger one at a fraction of what it had been worth when Alice became chief executive.

Having failed in her family banking business, Alice was offered a chance to run a paper-mill company. (An old friend of her father's interceded on her behalf.) Instead of being grateful, she told the chairman of the board who tried to recruit her that she would not take the job unless she was given a car and a chauffeur. Even after running the family business into the ground, she didn't see that her arrogance was her biggest enemy.

Alice should have accepted the job and worked hard for her new employer and the stockholders. In the process, she would have proven to herself that the initial failure was an aberration and that she was, indeed, a competent businesswoman.

3. Am I driven by pure greed? If you are only in it for the money, you will fail. As Confucius said, "A superior person understands righteousness, while an inept individual understands only profit."

Whenever your motive changes from serving others to greed, you will know your actions are not in line with Tao—and failure is inevitable. Here's an example.

Gloria was the general manager for a five-star hotel in Asia. This particular hotel had a beautiful marble floor covering a lobby that was large enough to hold an ice-skating rink. It used to have sofas, tables, and chairs in an area where hotel guests could wait and greet their guests. The lobby was always full of people, and business was good.

Even though the hotel had a huge coffee shop, as part of a re-modeling project, the management turned the lobby into two coffee lounges and removed the waiting area. If people wished to sit, they had to buy coffee at nine U.S. dollars a cup. Each refill was also nine dollars, and the waiters constantly pushed patrons to purchase snacks and desserts while they were sipping their coffee. A casual business meeting for four people, with tax and tip included, could easily cost more than one hundred U.S. dollars.

It was clear that Gloria had made her decision to eliminate the lobby for only one reason: greed. Gloria's obvious motive was to maximize her revenues. She did not have her guests' well-being in mind.

> Profitability is the goal of every business. However, short-term profit can come at the cost of long-term success.

Although I was a friend of Gloria's and had been a frequent guest at this hotel, often spending forty to sixty nights a year there, I found the new practice disturbing and refused to stay there. I could not support a hotel that would not allow my guests to sit with me in the lobby without charging a toll.

Apparently, I was not the only one who didn't like being held hostage by management's greed. Three years after Gloria put into practice her "no-free-seat" policy, the hotel closed one of the two coffee lounges and once again created an area where people could sit and talk. Not surprisingly, business has picked up.

4. *Am I desperate?* If you are downbeat, discouraged, depressed, or desperate, it is impossible to come up with successful strategies and ideas. When you're anxious, it is best to do nothing until you can let your anxiety go so that harmony, hope, and optimism—the characteristics of Tao—can be restored. When you hear your mind chanting "I want. I want. I must have," stop. Take a breath and try to gain some perspective. Pretend your life and the work you are doing are someone else's—and your desperation will vanish. The more you act from desperation, the less likely you will succeed.

5. *Who will be served and who will be hurt?* The more people you serve, and the fewer you hurt, the greater your success.

Some large companies use their resources trying to trap customers into accepting unfair agreements with fine print that is impossible to read without a microscope.

However, in time, consumers get smart. They figure out which company is trying to scam them and which truly wants to serve them. Trying to "hook" people for profit will ultimately drive customers away.

Providing a true and useful service to your fellow man (and woman) is the only legitimate path to long-term success.

The next story about a Taiwanese executive illustrates this point perfectly.

Wun Yu Chen, the retired chairman of Known-You Seed Co., Ltd., the inventor of the Santa brand cherry tomato, the seedless watermelon, and over two hundred watermelon varieties, built his fortune in the 1960s to 1980s with a booming Taiwan-based business.

In the 1990s he was approached by the Thai government to produce vegetable seeds and fruit in the poor section of northern Thailand. He agreed to do so.

"I made this decision because I wanted to help the Thai people improve their living conditions," Mr. Chen told me. "I went into the project thinking 'if I make money, great' but if I lose it, then so be it."

His motive wasn't to make more money; it was to lessen the suffering of humanity. But because he ran his business in accordance with Tao, the move has proved most lucrative.

For the last fifteen years, Taiwan has been repeatedly hit by typhoons, wiping out his seed crops there.

"Without the Thailand operation, we would be out of business," Mr. Chen says. Instead, his business consistently turned out a profit.

By attempting to save the Thai people from poverty, Mr. Chen also saved himself.

6. *What is the Tao of my job?* Your Tao, when it comes to your work, is to give it absolutely everything that you have *at all times.* Think of your paycheck as an agreement to support your employer.

Every time I say this to an audience of women, I am asked a series of "but what if . . ." questions. Let me address the most common:

But what if my boss is an idiot? Do I still have to give him 100 percent?

Your employer may not be all that you would wish him to be. But that very fact means he needs you even more.

But what if I hate my job?

If you don't like your job and your company, quit. (But line up another job first; it is always easier to find a job if you already have one.)

If you choose to stay, you don't have the right to sabotage the company through your constant expressions of dissatisfaction. If you don't have a solution to the problem you are complaining about, it is best to keep your mouth shut.

But what if I don't agree with the ethics of my company?

Quit. You are not obligated to help the unethical excel. But if you continue to accept a paycheck, you are explicitly endorsing the way your company does business.

The Right Decision, Every Time

It's natural to want to be promoted quickly and make more money. But that doesn't mean you should turn your back on your code of ethics.

While we can never fully protect ourselves against untimely disasters, we can protect ourselves against our own wrongdoing. Being ethical and in line with Tao is the foundation for any woman's career and the insurance policy that protects us from taking potentially harmful shortcuts. (Because there are no shortcuts. For every "overnight success" there are years of hard work that go unseen.)

By cheerfully aligning your objectives with Tao, you will make the right decision every time. You may not be an overnight success, but when you make it to the top, you will be able to look back on your actions with pride.

1.2

Tien (Timing)
From Universal to Personal Timing

The sun provides short and long days, and
the moon has waxing and waning cycles.

There are two kinds of timing. One is personal timing—control over whether you make a move or decision or not. I will discuss this concept later in the book.

The other is universal timing, which occurs when all the forces of nature are flowing in one direction. Neither you nor I can manipulate it, but we certainly can take advantage of it.

Being in sync with universal timing is like running with the wind at your back. It gives you the advantage of momentum, and momentum gives power. When you are aligned with an idea whose time has come, you are unstoppable. The good news is, the farther women progress into this new millennium, the more powerful we will become.

Where We Were and Where We Are

History is written by the victors. And there is no doubt that in the "war" between men and women, it has been men—up until now—who have been victorious. That's why women have gotten such short shrift in world history.

But today, after more than five thousand years of inequality, we are finally moving toward equality between men and women. So it is not surprising that the accomplishments of women—both past and present—are getting more attention. It is the way of Tao. As Lao Tzu put it, "The Universe, carrying Yin and Yang in Her bosom, infuses both forces with equal energy. Thus, harmony is created."

Sun Tzu understood this as well:

> Heaven is signified by Yin and Yang, manifested as summer and winter and the changing of the four seasons.

With the beginning of the new millennium, a new era is coming to the fore. We are truly moving away from history, toward her-story.

1.3

Di (Resources)
Turn Your Liabilities into Assets

> The earth contains far and near, danger and ease, open ground and narrow passes. These will determine your chance of life or death.

While the word *di* literally means "earth," Sun Tzu uses the concept more broadly to include many kinds of terrain, including flat land and mountains, rivers, and marshes.

On the battlefield, a general must take into account not only his or her opponent but also the terrain on which the battle will be fought. Invariably, the battleground will present both advantages and disadvantages.

On the positive side, there may be caves to hide in and narrow mountain passes that set the stage for a perfect ambush. But it is also possible that the general will be confronted with a river immediately ahead and mountains behind, making it difficult to lead troops forward.

No general can alter the surrounding terrain, no matter how much it stands in the way of victory. But he or she can understand it—and learn how to make the best of that which is beyond control.

It is no different at work. It doesn't matter if your boss, colleagues, employees, or clients love you, or if you work for a boss who takes credit for your work or a company that rarely promotes from within. You cannot change your company—at least not right away. But you *can* find a way to use the company's culture to your advantage. The key is knowing yourself, which is precisely what this book will teach you to do.

Turning "Liabilities" into Assets

The first and most important bit of terrain to take into account exists inside your head. If you do not take time to truly think about your strengths and weaknesses, you cannot begin to deal effectively with the external terrain you face.

How well you deal with your colleagues, bosses, employees, and clients—and your career in general—depends on how well you utilize your resources: both your positive and negative attributes.

As Sun Tzu said, Di will determine whether you will live or die. On the battlefield, a river is neither positive or negative. It all depends on how the general makes use of it in the course of a battle.

It is the same with your personal characteristics. No attribute is purely positive or negative. It all depends on what you do with the hand you have been dealt.

Everyone's life is filled with a certain number of liabilities. Yet these so-called disadvantages can be turned into secret weapons for winning.

Let's talk about how that can come about.

Turning Your Liabilities into Assets

1. *Know who you are.* It is possible to compete in a man's world and still enjoy being a woman. You can enjoy having a male coworker open your doors without feeling that your power has been diminished. Or perhaps you feel more comfortable opening it for him. It's your choice, and you should not feel you need to act one way or another because of what you believe is expected—or not expected—of you. By being competitive yet elegant, effective yet gentle, you will confuse, fascinate, and surprise your male coworkers and bosses.

Whatever your personal qualities are—aggressive or genteel; elegant or sporty; collaborative or competitive—don't be afraid to use them.

REFLECTION

Before you go any further, take some time to jot down and think about your unique qualities. (Hint: A friend or trusted coworker may be able to help you with this.)

_____

_____

_____

_____

_____

_____

2. *Blossom where you were planted.* Every experience that we have—both good and bad—helps shape who we are. Nothing is wasted. Oprah Winfrey is the perfect example. Her phenomenal success as a talk show host and media entrepreneur grew directly out of the life she had lived. As Merrell Noden relates in *Oprah Winfrey* (People Profiles, Time, Inc.), Winfrey was born into poverty, grew up surrounded by bigotry, and got pregnant (but lost the baby) when she was fourteen. All she experienced in early life contributed to her sensitivity and enhanced her ability to relate to others. She blossomed where she was planted.

3. *Find a fresh perspective.* It does not matter who you are or what kind of product or service you sell; be the first to explore and execute outrageous and unconventional strategies.

This is an especially useful strategy when you find yourself at a disadvantage. The typical reaction when you find yourself in an inferior position is to try to appear as if you are more powerful than you are. Not so Golda Meir, former prime minister of Israel, as one scene in the award-winning docudrama *Golda* revealed:

Desperately needing America to supply her with military arms and equipment in the aftermath of the Six-Day War in 1967, she entertained members of the U.S. Armed Services Committee at her home.

Now, Meir had many things working against her.

1. She was the prime minister of a small country.

2. She was old.

3. Her country was constantly being threatened by its Muslim neighbors.

Instead of putting on airs, Meir served the visiting congressional delegation tea and slices of her homemade cake, foisting second and third helpings on them like, well, a Jewish grandmother.

By acting like a gracious elderly host instead of a prime minister, she charmed her guests—and got the members of the committee to agree to her request.

After all, how can anyone say no to a grandmother when she asks for a few jets and missiles?

Instead of waiting for someone else to blaze a new trail or to find a new way of doing things, do it yourself. I guarantee it will pay off. But be careful. Don't do anything just to be outrageous. Whatever you choose to do should be a natural extension of your personality, or it will definitely backfire.

As Sun Tzu says:

> In a battle, use your regular formations to engage the enemy. Use unexpected surprises to overcome them.

4. *Understand that your so-called liabilities can be your assets.* Our troubles start with the way we define liabilities and assets. Liabilities are established by the majority in any given culture; but the same liability in one culture would be considered an asset in another.

Let me give you a personal example. Many Asians have said to me, "We've heard the United States is a place that discriminates against Asians as well as women. You have two strikes against you. How do you handle it?"

My answer is "Being an Asian woman has proven to be my strength, not my weakness. If I were a blue-eyed, blond male and had gone to the same schools and learned the same things that they had, I wouldn't know how to set myself apart. It is tough to compete with people who are identical to you. Being different gives me an edge."

Of course, if I were a blond, blue-eyed male, I would have had to discover the things that would make me stand out. Everyone has them. Being different is not a liability; it makes you unique.

5. Change your circumstances, so your liabilities become your strengths. There's no point trying to fit a round peg into a square hole. If you discover that your job requires you to be creative, but you prefer analytical tasks to coming up with outrageous ideas, you might want to rethink your career. That doesn't mean you can't thrive in a creative working environment. Maybe your ability to stay on task can help your team finish projects that otherwise would have dragged on for months. But if it is not possible to integrate your own strengths into your current job, it's probably time to dust off the résumé.

If you become an accountant, architect, or logistical engineer, your "liabilities" at your old profession would instantly be transformed into strengths. After all, these days especially, no company wants a creative accountant.

> An understanding of how to turn our liabilities into strengths can result in an endless string of possibilities.

6. On the other side of your strengths lie your weaknesses.

The universe contains five elements: water, fire, wood, metal, earth.

Water can conquer fire, wood, and metal. Yet earth can conquer water.

The same principle goes for fire, wood, metal, and earth.

In each element's strength lies its weakness.

Just as your liabilities can become your assets, so can your assets become your liabilities.

As Sun Tzu wrote:

> Out of orderliness comes chaos. Out of courage
> comes cowardice. Out of strength comes weakness.

If your strength is empathy and compassion, then you might be prone to weakness or ineptitude when it comes to disciplining your staff.

If you are opinionated and quick to make decisions, you may also be intolerant and inflexible.

If you are very confident, you can come across as arrogant.

Let me give you an example of what I am talking about.

Jessica, a young media professional, has always been praised for her ability to get along with anyone and to put her own needs behind the needs of the people she works with. Yet, as she is now learning, her selflessness has come with a price: She's spent so much time helping other people that she's neglected taking the necessary steps to advance her own career.

She has a choice. She can continue trying to please everyone—and remain unfulfilled in her own career—or she can take an active step toward making her own career take off. The choice is Jessica's to make.

Be proud of your strengths. (Getting along with people is certainly a good thing.) But don't forget to pay attention to how your strengths may simultaneously be working against you.

The definitions of "strength" and "weakness" are not one-dimensional. We have to consider our personal attributes and life experiences, and use them to turn our strengths and weaknesses upside down and inside out.

As a strong general, you must learn to use whatever geographic terrain you come across to your advantage. As a strong woman, you should take a close look at what people have labeled your liabilities. In them you may find powerful weapons.

REFLECTION

Make a list of your strengths and your weaknesses. Challenge your mind to use them in a way that you've never used them before. For example, maybe you have a tendency to daydream on the job. Now stretch your mind to turn those liabilities into strengths. With a little hard work and patience, you can turn your daydreams into reality—and even a source of earning power.

STRENGTHS   **WEAKNESSES**

_____   _____

_____   _____

_____   _____

_____   _____

_____   _____

_____   _____

_____   _____

_____   _____

_____   _____

_____   _____

_____   _____

_____   _____

_____   _____

1.4

Jiang (Leadership)
A State of Mind

*The commander must be wise, trustful,
benevolent, courageous, and strict.*

True leadership *(Jiang)* is not about your job title; it is all about
your attitude. We women seldom see ourselves as leaders. And
yet every woman has at some point assumed the role, even if she
has never held a senior management position—or even worked
in a company.

Growing up, you may have taken care of your siblings; today
you may lead a church group, PTA, or charity. We often don't
think of this as leadership, we think of it as the stuff of everyday
life. But it is indeed leadership.

A woman in her twenties listened to me say this during a
speech and then raised her hand during the question-and-answer
session.

"You make it sound simple," she said. "But I just don't feel
comfortable leading. I don't think I have ever been in charge of
anything in my life."

But, it turned out, she had. After my speech we had coffee
and she told me about an incident that occurred during a recent
vacation; she and her boyfriend had been stranded at a seaside
restaurant with no way to get back into town.

"I called for a cab and was told one would be coming any
minute, but an hour later, we were still waiting," she told me.
"There were shuttle buses nearby that would take people back

to their hotels, but they refused to leave until they were full, and even including the two of us there were only a handful of people on the bus.

"After waiting around another fifteen minutes, it dawned on me that this was all wrong. I got up and walked around the restaurant asking who was waiting for a cab. It turns out thirty people were. I explained how the shuttle buses worked and I got all of them to get on. We were back downtown in fifteen minutes."

"See," I told her, "that's all there is to it. You didn't wait for permission. You did something because you knew nothing gets done unless you have a leader."

The fact that most people don't see themselves as leaders means more opportunities for you. If we want to make the twenty-first century the Woman's Century, we cannot wait to be called "leaders." We must naturally embrace the role. When you're in a situation that requires leadership, take the reins. Don't sit around and wait, as this senior vice president did:

Robin had steadily worked her way up through the public relations industry and at the age of forty-seven found herself senior vice president of communications for a Fortune 100 company. But she had little respect for the man she reported to, the head of marketing. He was lazy and spent most of his day trying to figure out what would make the CEO happy, instead of trying to determine what would be best for the company.

Robin sent memos to her boss outlining both new marketing campaigns and potential new areas where the company could expand, only to find them ignored. She knew she could do a better job, if only someone would let her.

When her boss died of a sudden heart attack, Robin waited and waited for the CEO to promote her, but six months later the marketing position remained vacant. Instead of filling in where she could—which, of course, would have raised her profile—or going directly to the CEO with her plans, she simply went about running the communications department the best she could, certain that eventually someone would give her a chance to lead the entire marketing department.

When a new head of marketing was named almost a year later, all Robin did was complain to her friends about how unfairly she had been treated. She did not realize that she had blown the opportunity to step in and start leading.

> The way you lead is simply by leading.

What Leadership Is Not

Leadership is not about brute force but about inner strength and direction; it is not a behavior, it is a focus. We can be gentle leaders at home and firm-handed leaders at work. Anyone who has empathy and understanding, who can earn the trust of those being led and can provide direction, is a good leader.

1.5

Fa (Managing)
It Is All About Execution

Your army must be well organized and clearly carry out the command signals; disciplined in performing its duty and responsibilities according to ranks; masterful in supply of material resources and controlled in its military spending.

In large part the rest of the book is devoted to Fa, "discipline" or "managing." We will be discussing how you can manage your staff; how you can manage your relations with your boss; and even how you can manage your interactions with colleagues.

Before we go any further, though, let's touch on the first bit of managing that must be done before you can attempt any of those things. How will you manage the relationship between your work and personal life?

Traditionally, the work-life balance discussion always seems to boil down to the idea of "having it all." We women can either have it all, or, if we listen to the media, we are missing something.

But the reality is that it is not about "having it all." It is about doing what makes you happy. If what gives you the most joy in life is being a top executive, you will not be happy focusing the majority of your energy on your family. Conversely, if you really want to be at home with your family, you are never going to be fulfilled at work. You need to be true to yourself.

But it is possible to want—and have—it all. It's simply a matter of recognizing that "having it all" means something different to different people.

REFLECTION

Make a list of the ten things you want most out of life—the things you believe will bring you true joy and fulfillment. As you read the rest of this book, keep them in mind. Don't forget that this is what you're working for.

_____

_____

_____

_____

1.6

Deception
Appear Weak When You Are Strong

The essence of war is deception.

Deception is the last essential point in the first chapter of *The Art of War*. It's about appearing weak if you are strong, close when you are far away, and creating situations where you bring out your enemy's worst traits in order to defeat him.

We will see examples of all of the following points throughout the book, but for now let's just touch on some of the ways you might employ deception.

1. If a colleague is jealous of you, appear less threatening than you are to avoid her assault and save your job. Let's say you and a colleague—the daughter of a key customer—are after the same promotion.

She may be more connected, but it is clear that you are more qualified. In this case, you should not appear to threaten her directly. Don't show off your smart ideas at meetings that you both attend; she just might steal them. Save your brilliance until you have one-on-one meetings with your boss. Remember, you don't need to prove yourself to *her.*

2. Don't show off. Let people discover you. You do not have to work hard to get attention. Work hard at your job instead, and people will notice. Voice your opinion only when the situation calls for it. If you are as smart as you think you are, your brilliance will come through. I am not suggesting silence. If you have brilliant ideas, assert yourself—but do so at the right time and in the right way. Be professional. Don't brag or point out how clever you are. Get support from the right people before presenting your ideas to the entire organization. Otherwise, you are not likely to get many more chances.

3. Be careful of radical ideas. If your idea is extreme, proceed with caution.

People—and organizations—are generally afraid of risk. Before you present a wild idea, ask yourself: Is my boss risk-averse? Is my company? If so, you may need to wait until you have a new boss, or the company is in trouble, or the overall market changes before your revolutionary idea is accepted. If you propose the idea at the wrong time, or to the wrong person, it may be rejected simply because people are afraid of change. Find out who in your organization embraces change instead. After all, companies that change with the times get noticed.

Consider one of today's most successful newcomers in the banking business, Washington Mutual. Instead of following the traditional conservative banking model, with dignified and formal interiors, Washington Mutual set up new branches as inviting and comfortable as a Starbucks shop. Branches contain a children's play area and, to draw in younger customers, they've offered cash and gift incentives for setting up new accounts. All of these choices go against the grain of traditional banking, but the universal timing was right for Washington Mutual. Banks were in desperate need of a makeover, and Washington Mutual stepped in at just the right moment.

4. Do not feign stupidity. There is a cultural difference between China and the West. In China, people assume that you are smarter than you make yourself out to be. They try to see beyond the facade, your hidden brilliance. In the West, the typical boss won't work that hard. If you come off as unintelligent, he or she will assume that you are. Once your boss starts to think of you that way, it will be very difficult to change his or her mind.

5. *If you still have a lot to learn, keep your mouth shut.* If you rarely speak, people won't know how inexperienced you are. (And, as in China, some people may think you know more than you do!)

6. *Deception has two natures; one is offensive, the other defensive.* The first five points dealt with how you can use deception offensively, how you can subtly deceive people about your true power. But you also need to know how to deal with people who are trying to deceive you.

In other words, beware of the wolf in sheep's clothing.

Knowing What to Reveal

As I said at the beginning, Master Sun's philosophy is a holistic one.

His view on deception is a prime example. You need to understand who you are—how smart, how aggressive—as well as who your colleagues and competitors are. If you know what you are dealing with, you'll know how much of yourself to reveal.

CHAPTER 2

Doing Battle
Speedy Victory

here is an old Chinese saying, one that Sun Tzu was likely aware of, that goes: *Shang chang ru zhan chang.* This phrase literally translates to "the marketplace is a battlefield," and it explains how the Chinese view the nature of business competition: The success of a company influences the survival and well-being of its employees and stockholders, as surely as the course of a battle determines a nation's fate.

At the personal level, we are all competing for better jobs. There is simply not enough space on the top of the pyramid for everyone who wants to work there.

It is not enough for women to demand professional equality. We can't say, "I am a woman, so I deserve to be treated equally." Whether you are a man or woman, you need to earn respect.

And nothing speaks louder than bringing in profit for the

company. Only when you bring in money like a queen will you be treated like a queen.

Earning your keep is what this chapter is all about. As you will discover, Sun Tzu provides a results-oriented, cost-effective strategy on how to win on the battlefield with the minimum amount of effort.

2.1

Eat What You Kill

One who is skilled in warfare . . . will not depend on the food supplies that are transported from the distant home country.

What Master Sun meant by this is that, while the home country supplies an army's military equipment, the food for the troops should be gathered from the enemy's warehouses.

Transporting provisions over a long distance costs money— thus directly affecting the people of the nation through increased taxes, a depletion of resources, and the like.

How does this principle apply to us? In essence, Master Sun is talking about the importance of resourcefulness. It's not enough just to show up to the office every day and put in face time. You need to create results if you want to keep your job, let alone get promoted. Let me explain how you can do just that.

1. *Your "personal bottom line."* Your company should provide you with all the necessary tools and training in order for you to win the battle of the marketplace.

It's up to you, however, to put them to good use. To put it plainly, you need to generate far more income for your company than what you are paid.

Few people start off in a position to generate money directly—if you have a support staff or assistant's position, for example, your Tao is to work effectively; if you give your employer more than he or she is paying for, eventually you will be rewarded. In fact, there's no better way to move forward in your career. A successful young woman recently shared that she knew she had reached a more important stage in her career because suddenly she wasn't as concerned about her own title or salary; she'd begun thinking about making money for her company. She knew that her own success was directly linked to her "company bottom line."

If you remember this, you will always be valuable. If you don't, your employers will find someone else who does.

2. Provide for yourself and *others.* As the Chinese proverb says, "The nature of war is the battle of money." In other words, it takes a lot of money to fight a battle.

Running a company also takes a lot money. If you are hoping to advance within your organization, you must keep that point in mind.

On your desk, in addition to the picture of your kids, lover, or husband, place a picture of your whole department—maybe even a photo that shows your entire company. You are working for them as well.

3. Reward results. This is something that Sun Tzu understood well.

In order to motivate your troops to capture the enemy's provisions, you need to reward them with profit. During the battle of the charioteers, whoever first captures ten enemy charioteers should be honored and highly rewarded to stimulate the morale.

Share generously with those who work for you. For those special individuals who make great contributions to the company's financial well-being, acknowledge them with monetary rewards, bonuses, prestigious titles, promotions, and honors. If you don't, someone else will.

Michelle was working for an international accounting firm and was stationed in Paris. She was creative, aggressive, and hard-working—the kind of worker any company would be proud to have. In the last fiscal year, she had put together several large international deals and had made her company $20 million. For her outstanding performance, she received a mere $2,000 bonus.

She quit. Now she is running her own company. Last year it grossed $100 million.

If you are just starting your career, you may not be able to quit your job to open a new company that will gross $100 million. However, your brilliance will be noticed in time—if not by your boss, then by others. But remember, if at all possible, always find a new job before you quit your old one.

> In order to ensure your own survival, generously reward those who bring in results.

If you don't liberally reward your superior performers, most likely you will end up creating your own competition. If your employers aren't rewarding your superior performance, become the competition.

4. *Sell yourself first.* Here is the way Master Sun articulated this concept:

> She will win when her superior does not
> interfere with her campaign.

In order to conduct effective warfare, a general needs the freedom to make decisions on the battlefield instead of having to listen to orders from the faraway court.

Similarly, the only way you can insure that your superior (your boss) will give you a free hand to do your best work is if you have successfully convinced him or her that you can get the job done.

If you haven't earned his or her confidence by performing at a superior level, your boss cannot help but interfere.

No matter what your job or title, you need to sell yourself first. Until you have convinced the world that you are worthy of great things, don't expect to be given much responsibility.

(What most people don't realize is that it is actually much easier to sell yourself than it is to sell any product or idea. You usually have little control over a product or service you're selling or a project you're working on. Often it was the result of a team effort or was created by a group of people you don't know. You, on the other hand, have complete control over your own life.)

How you represent yourself affects every aspect of your life: from getting a job to making a sale, enjoying a healthy relationship to gaining respect and love from your children.

If you haven't made an effort to improve yourself physically or mentally by taking the right actions and thinking the right thoughts, it will show. It will be hard to sell yourself and even harder to sell your product. People do business with those whom they like and believe in.

Sharing the Spoils

Make yourself invaluable by bringing in projects, clients, and ideas that no one else can. How can anyone discriminate against you at the office—or anywhere else, for that matter—when their survival depends on you?

In the last chapter, you created a list of your unique traits. Think about those traits once again, but this time, figure out how to use them to sell yourself. How can you use your talents to bring in clients or ideas that no one else in your company can? How can you use them to generate real profits for your company?

_____

_____

_____

_____

_____

_____

_____

_____

_____

_____

2.2

Close the Deal Fast

The most important element of conducting warfare is aiming
for a swift victory and avoiding a prolonged campaign.

A military victory that uses up all of your resources isn't much of a victory. Neither is spending years trying to land a meager job or a small contract that won't make you happy.

In other words, not only do you want to win the battle, you want to make sure it is worth fighting.

Be Valuable to Your Employer

The faster you can close deals, the more valuable you will appear to your employer. Every company wants new sources of revenue coming in as quickly as possible and will reward the employees who can make it happen.

Helen, a sales executive for a high-tech company in the San Francisco Bay area, was very good at generating new business leads and networking with everyone from Tokyo to London. But her boss, Terry, began to notice that whenever it came time to close the deal, Helen would let the contract sit around on her desk for weeks—sometimes even forgetting about it—while she was busy drumming up fresh new leads.

Terry reminded Helen that each time she went after new leads, it cost the company a lot in international telephone calls, not to speak of the time and labor required. All Helen needed to do to make the time and energy she put into generating new leads worthwhile was to follow through. But instead she neglected the contracts that were sitting right on top of her desk— things that would bring money into the firm immediately.

The conversation forced Helen to understand something about herself. She loved conducting the battle—finding out what customers needed and figuring out how to satisfy them before the competition did—much more than doing all the paperwork required to make the deal happen.

Realizing this, she convinced her boss to hire someone to handle all the paperwork for her. Helen went on to become a top producer in her industry.

The Tao of Closing the Deal

1. Know your product. You need to have an honest assessment of your product's strengths and weaknesses, so that you can answer any question thrown at you. If you are selling real estate, for example, you have to know not only about the house you are selling, but also about the area in which it is located and the current market.

2. Know your customer. What does he or she need? To continue with the real estate scenario, is he or she ready to buy or just beginning the process of purchasing a home? Couples with children want homes in areas with good schools; young buyers might be more interested in how trendy the area is; and investors will want to know whether prices in that neighborhood are going up or down.

3. Does your product fit the customer's needs? Is there a way to make it fit, if it doesn't immediately appear as if it does? For example, is it possible to add a fourth bedroom, if that is what the purchaser wants, or can one of the bedrooms be turned into a home office?

4. Ask for the business by simply asking for it. If potential buyers really like the house you have shown them, ask if they are ready to make an offer.

5. Solve the customer's problem. It's the easiest way to close the deal. Avon is not selling another moisturizer. It is selling something that will make you happy by helping you to appear younger and more appealing.

Or, as Harvard Business School professor Ted Levitt put it to his marketing students: "You are not selling a quarter-inch drill bit, you are selling quarter-inch holes."

The example I've offered comes from the world of sales, but that's certainly not the only field these lessons apply to. No matter what kind of business you're in, you're selling something and you have some kind of client. Figuring out what you have and what other people need is the key to any business transaction.

What Works in Business Works in Life

Of course, this lesson doesn't apply only to business.

The close-the-deal-fast principle also extends to your personal life. If you have been dating someone for an eternity, and the relationship still has not escalated (and you want it to), you need to expedite your closing as you would any business transaction.

First, determine why you have not been able to close the deal. There could be many reasons why things have gotten stuck. For example, your significant other:

a. Might have been hurt in the past

b. Could feel that the relationship is perfect the way it is

c. Might not believe in marriage—at least not in marriage with you

d. Might not be ready

If, even after talking things through, you realize there is no hope in closing the deal, you need to move on.

Whether in business or your personal life, it is important to close the deals that you can and drop those deals that you cannot. When you are preoccupied with the deals that you have no hope of closing, you prevent yourself from seeing other opportunities.

REFLECTION

Even if you are not a salesperson, your job requires you to close deals, whether it is getting someone to return your phone calls, following through on projects you are developing, or closing the loop on an outstanding request. What deals are you currently trying to close? Is there something you can do to speed up the process? What unique quality do you possess that might allow you to close the loop? What is your customer or client looking for—and how can you give it to him or her?

CHAPTER 3

Strategy
Know Thyself and Others

On the corporate battlefield, your opponent may be one person—a rival within your company, perhaps—or hundreds of thousands—such as the employees at a competing company.

But no matter the number, there are only two sides in the battle: you and them.

Clearly, you want to know what the other side is going to do. If they are going to attack, you must be ready to defend. If they are going to introduce a new product, you'll need to counter with one of your own.

But before you can do any of that, you need to take a giant step back. Understanding the opposition begins with understanding yourself. Why? Because you filter all the information about others through your own lens—one that is already clouded by your own thoughts and experiences. You will see examples of how this works, both positively and negatively, throughout this chapter.

As Lao Tzu, on whose philosophy Sun Tzu's strategy was built, said, "Knowing others is wisdom; knowing yourself is enlightenment."

If you don't know yourself, then all your information about others will be interpreted improperly; it will be distorted and quite possibly defective, putting you at a huge disadvantage once the battle begins.

There are two other reasons you need to know yourself, before you can try to understand others.

How well you know the world around you is directly proportional to how well you know yourself.

First, as I have explained, Master Sun's philosophy is a holistic one; in his view, all the actions in the universe are interconnected. Because everything flows from the same source, self-understanding increases your understanding of others.

Second, when you are very familiar with your shortcomings (whether you're quick to anger, prone to jealousy, full of self-doubt, or afraid to fail), you will be more understanding when you see them in other people.

These qualities are what make us human. In fact, because they are so common, the next time you're talking to someone, try reading facial expressions to determine his or her emotional state so you can act accordingly. You'll probably know how he or she is feeling before a word is said. Why? Because you have experienced those same emotions yourself.

Five Steps to Knowing Yourself and Others

Know yourself and your counterpart; even after a hundred battles you will not feel trapped and in danger.

If you are clueless about your counterpart, but you only know yourself, the chance for victory is fifty-fifty.

If you know neither others nor yourself, one hundred battles, one hundred defeats.

In today's business world, the "counterparts" that Sun Tzu is talking about include your boss, staff, suppliers, customers, distributors, board members, investors, competitors, and anyone who is a part of your business dealings.

In your personal life, they would include your husband or partner, children, parents, relatives, and friends.

But no matter whom you are dealing with, if you don't understand *yourself,* the interactions you have with *everyone else* will be flawed every time. The flaws may be big or small, but I can guarantee that if you don't know them, *all* your interactions will be missing something. Without self-awareness, dealing with other people is like target shooting in the dark.

How Can You Not Know Yourself? It's Easy!

At first blush, the idea that you could not know yourself sounds ridiculous. But the odds are, you don't. We aren't talking about the superficial stuff, like the way you wear your hair or your taste in music. The "real you" I'm talking about means the way you react to difficult situations, what you worry about, and how you view the world—the things that help or hurt you in your business and personal life.

If you don't know this "real you," you are bound to make the same mistakes over and over again; before long you might find yourself on the treadmill labeled "professional victim." You know the type—the people who say "Why does the world always pick on me?" without questioning their own behavior.

Annette is an investment banker who raises money for movie projects. She is a chronic liar, but she doesn't think of herself that way. She doesn't even think she is a liar. To her, the falsehoods are just clever maneuvering.

If she promises you ten things, at best she may deliver one. As for the rest, she functions as a brilliant novelist, weaving very complicated stories to explain why she didn't do what she promised. She will never come out and say she simply did not keep her word.

The easiest solution for someone like this, of course, is not to commit to doing so many things. But because Annette does not realize her proclivities for falsehoods, that idea never presents itself. As a result, she just continues to lie to explain why she doesn't get things done, and she is always amazed that people who have dealt with her in the past don't trust her to keep her word. As a banker, her words have to be golden. She has to be honest about what she can or cannot do. After a client of mine worked with her for one year, he left with the impression that she was a con woman. I think differently—I believe she just has a tendency to bite off more than she can chew. Nevertheless, until she takes a good look at her work style, her business partners will continue to have a negative view of her.

Are Women Good at Knowing Themselves?

In my experience, women are more sensitive than men, more intuitive, and more adept at spotting the shortcomings of others (especially their own spouses!). But, when it comes to having a true understanding of ourselves, we don't always score so high.

It's not that men are any better. In fact, most of us, men and women alike, are weak in this area. It isn't surprising; we've had years and years of reading, writing, and arithmetic, but we were never trained to learn about ourselves. Yet knowing yourself is essential for you to be effective in your business and life encounters. It's time to learn.

Let me use an extreme example to make the point. If a saleswoman who doesn't understand herself gets rejected all the time, she is likely to think there is something wrong with her. Of course, that is nonsense. Rejection is part of sales. If a good saleswoman hears twenty nos in one day, she doesn't give up; she just says, "Okay, I'll make the sale to the twenty-first customer!"

But if you don't understand that the customers who say no aren't rejecting you personally—if you make no distinction between friends who turn you down and customers who do—you will spend all your time at work feeling hurt.

Knowing yourself makes it far easier to go through life. You're better equipped to interpret events and other people. You're better able to separate real problems from ones that are just in your mind. You understand that people are rejecting your sales pitch because they don't need your product, not because you are a bad person.

Most of us desperately wanted to be part of the "in crowd" in high school, but few of us were. As a result, we felt rejected and hurt. Having a customer say no can tap into the same feelings we had back then.

But though the feelings are the same, the cause is totally different. Kids can be cruel for no reason. A customer who says no to your company's chocolates may simply be on a diet.

Intellectually, we know a customer who rejects our product offerings is not rejecting us personally. Understanding that *emotionally* is different. If you know yourself, and recognize why this particular situation is triggering deeper feelings of rejection and pain, the situation becomes easier to deal with.

Seeing, They See Not

A superior businessperson knows what a customer or client wants, even if he or she can't express it. An understanding mother can sense something is wrong with her child. A considerate woman can detect whether her spouse had a good day at work. You can't always depend on others to tell you what they need from you; often they can't tell you, or they don't know themselves because they are not in touch with their feelings.

But how can you know what your customer, colleague, or spouse wants if you don't know what *you* want? You cannot even begin to *think* of leading others until you know how to lead yourself. And you cannot lead yourself until you know yourself.

The following five steps can help you better understand yourself.

1. *You must have a strong desire to know yourself.* Most people—both men and women—do not recognize the need for self-examination until something terrible happens to them. These costly lessons are meant to give you a wake-up call. Once the smoke has cleared, if you are lucky, you will begin to see that it is necessary for *you* to understand what it is about you that is holding you back.

Here's an example. An acquaintance of mine, Maryann, wanted badly to lose weight and get fit. She joined a gym, began to exercise, and started eating well. After three or four days, she started to feel better. As soon as she did, she stopped exercising and rewarded herself with a huge, fattening meal with her friend Joe, followed by a movie with her friend Abby.

Maryann thought she wanted to have a better life. But she failed to realize how stuck in her old patterns she'd become. Feeling good actually made her feel uncomfortable, which sent her back to her old patterns.

Unless Maryann truly understands that, nothing is ever going to change.

2. *Be your own detective.* You can be your own detective and figure out who the real you is. Here's how Maryann did it.

As soon as she looked at how she'd been behaving, she began to see a pattern. It wasn't Joe's fault that she blew her diet when he asked her to dinner. And it wasn't Abby's fault for inviting her to a movie that happened at the same time as her dance class. Maryann hadn't made enough of a commitment to her new habits to keep the old ones from creeping back in.

If you constantly do things that betray your own goals, you need to find out why. Whom are you trying to please? What are the possible root causes or past incidents that are causing you to act this way? For example, if you were told as a child to be nice to everyone, you may find yourself betraying your own best interest by going along with others.

This very quality can hold you hostage throughout your life. It can show up as timidity when you have to give orders, discipline your staff, or make a decision about which of two potential projects to choose.

How often have you experienced an internal debate between your emotions and logic that goes something like this: "Yes, I am supposed to . . . but I don't feel comfortable doing it"? And how often have you actually examined where the conflict is coming from? If the answer is "rarely" or "never," you need to start immediately.

Given the importance of knowing yourself, why don't more people try to do it? The answer is that many people—at least subconsciously—don't want to know. They are afraid of what they may find out. After all, who really wants to know that they can be insecure and eager to please?

And yet we need to understand ourselves—warts and all—if we are ever going to understand others.

Conversely, being your own detective can help you stay in

the zone. We've all had days when we can do no wrong. We also need to stop and analyze why things went so well. Ignorance is *not* bliss; it's dangerous. Just as we need to discover all our fears and shortcomings if we are to overcome them, we can also learn the things that make us great.

Think of your mind as a detective who's constantly on surveillance. When you watch yourself long enough, your hidden nature will be revealed. And that brings me to the next point.

3. Dive into yourself. There is a primal state of self-knowledge that exists within each of us. We just have to find it.

One time, while vacationing in Florida, I became furious at my friend for shaking red pepper over the pizza we were sharing. I was so angry about this insignificant action that I walked out of the restaurant.

Even as I did so, I knew my anger had nothing to do with the pizza, because I was not even hungry. I needed to find out what was really bothering me, so I lay down on a bench in the garden outside the restaurant and looked into the starry winter sky, pondering.

It took an hour, but finally I had the answer. I had just begun a major project that everyone said would be wonderful for my career. I had never felt good about working with this particular client, but I talked myself into accepting the assignment.

Lying on that bench looking into the sky, I realized I had gotten upset because deep inside, I knew this project was the wrong thing to do. When I opened myself up to my inner guidance, all of my fury vanished. I was left with peace and certainty.

The next time you find yourself getting upset over something trivial, find a quiet place where you can think about what's *really* bothering you. Doing so will not only provide you with insight into yourself, it will also allow you to tap into wisdom you didn't even know you had. This kind of quiet reflection is the fastest way to dive into your center where peace, self-knowledge, and intuition dwell.

4. *See yourself through someone else's eyes.* Often others see us better than we see ourselves. Find someone who knows you well, someone who truly has your interests in mind, and ask how he or she sees you.

But be careful whom you ask to be your mirror. If the mirror is cracked, the reflection will be distorted. Here's an example of how this approach can work well when you ask a trusted friend to be your mirror.

When Denise, a Fortune 500 company CEO, divorced her first husband, a CEO at another firm, she said it was because the last thing she wanted to do after working all day was talk shop. When her second marriage failed (this time her husband was a poet), she said it was because he wanted her home every night, but she needed to work late and travel often.

When Denise complained about her ex-husbands to her childhood friend Jan, Jan replied, "You may know how to make millions for your company and yourself, but you are clueless when it comes to your life companions. You don't know what you want in a husband, or even if you want a husband at all."

Denise's reaction? "I can't believe it. You're right. It is so obvious, but I just couldn't see it!" She'd been so busy blaming her ex-husbands that she never stopped to think about her own shortcomings as a wife.

It's helpful to have a supportive friend to act as a mirror and reflect your true self back at you. At work, this kind of mentor or colleague is indispensable. Try asking someone you trust about your work style. What do they admire? Do they have suggestions about how you can improve? You may be surprised at their answers.

5. *Be an actor and director.* Live as if you are both the actor and the director of *Your Life, the Movie.*

Here's what I mean. If an actress does not perform well in rehearsals, the director will stop the scene and discuss how she can improve her performance. Then they will do the scene again. Lisa's story demonstrates how you can take the same approach.

Lisa is a project manager with a million-dollar budget. She plans her presentations thoroughly and rehearses until she knows the material cold. Yet every time she delivers a presentation, she stutters. Lisa, the actor, was struggling.

She turned to her inner director to find out why. When she did, she discovered that the root of her fear of public speaking was her deep desire to impress her boss. She desperately wanted him to see her as a shining star, one he had to promote.

The director inside told her not to worry about whether the boss would be impressed: "Just concentrate on communicating the material as clearly as possible."

She tried not to care about the boss's reaction during her next presentation, but it didn't work, because she still didn't know "how not to care." Her mind was telling her not to care, but emotionally she cared quite a bit. Not only was she proud of the material she was presenting, she desperately wanted to be recognized.

After more discussions with her inner director, she began imagining that her next presentation would be her last. She convinced herself that she would be leaving the company for a much better job, so the reaction to this presentation—the last one she would ever have to give to her employer—wouldn't matter.

This approach worked superbly for her. She used it the next few times she presented, and shortly thereafter she was promoted.

Lisa's fear is a common one. How many of us stumble in our current jobs because we're focused on what will happen next? Live every workday as if it were your last day on the job, and you'll be amazed at how focused and confident you'll be!

Knowing yourself is a lifetime commitment, but it's a crucial one. How well you know the world around you is directly related to how well you know yourself.

3.2

Create an Innovative Résumé to Sell Yourself

Thus a skilled warrior subdues enemy's troops without raising arms; captures cities without laying siege; destroys countries without lengthy warfare.

As I have said before, business is war, and our competitors are our opponents. Given the number and scope of our enemies, we can't fight them all head-to-head. It would be too exhausting. Therefore, we need to outmaneuver and outsmart them whenever possible. Hopefully, we can be clever enough that they will give up without a fight. Creating a clever résumé is one way to do that.

That is something Sun Tzu understood. Remember, he wrote *The Art of War* as a résumé to win a job with the King of Wu. His words were bold and confident: "The leader who listens to my strategy will surely win. Then I will stay here to serve him. The leader who does not adopt my strategy will surely lose."

Master Sun was trying to make himself look as important as possible on his résumé, and it worked.

The same sort of approach can work for you. If you understand your uniqueness, you can create extraordinary strategies to get ahead and gain advantages over others.

Your résumé should include all of your knowledge, wisdom,

aspiration, visions, and accomplishments that truly represent who you really are.

I'm not talking about a traditional one- to two-page résumé. How can you appear unique, if your presentation of yourself is the same as everyone else's?

That one- or two-page résumé is fine, and you might need it for certain interviews. But I'm not just talking about a piece of paper to show potential employers; what I'm referring to is what will *accompany* that piece of paper.

"My Résumé"

In 1987, I was working as an independent consultant in Portland, Oregon. One of my major clients, the State of Oregon, was looking for a way to help Oregon-based companies sell their products in China. I was very happy doing the work, until someone less experienced was appointed to oversee all Oregon-China relationships. To my dismay, he seemed to delight in trying to squeeze me out. Every night I went home crying.

But as I have learned, if you get hurt enough, eventually you learn. Suddenly it hit me. Why should I fight so hard to try to keep my position as a big fish in a very small fishpond? If I was as good as I thought, I should go to the ocean to prove myself.

Since I couldn't spend sixty hours explaining to each potential client how to do business with China—nobody will pay for that kind of extensive background—it made the most sense for me to write a book on the subject and let it serve as my résumé. (I may have subconsciously borrowed the idea from Sun Tzu.)

I had absolutely no idea how to create a book, but I figured the best way was to start writing. And so I did. The result was my first book, *The Chinese Mind Game,* which I published myself.

I intended to send it out to potential clients. But before I did, I approached several publications and asked them to review it. (Never brag about yourself when someone else can do it for you!) I got lucky. The book got rave reviews from *The San Francisco Chronicle* and, later, Britain's *Financial Times*. Suddenly I had companies from all over the world calling me and asking for copies of the book—and consulting help. Literary agents started knocking on my door, and eventually one sold the book to a major New York publisher. This started my career as an author.

A Unique Résumé Requires Some Soul-Searching

Creating a unique résumé requires you to look deep into your soul (the earlier chapters should have helped you begin doing this) to find what it is that makes you special. What skills do you possess that will make you stand out? What do you know that no one else does?

Only you know what these skills are. But you have them. No one sees the world exactly as you do.

Even if you are a twenty-four-year-old who's been working as an assistant for two years, you have skills. You can tell a future employer, as one young woman did, "I did the fastest coffee runs you had ever seen." Her sense of humor—and the fact that she took pride in performing the menial tasks assigned to her—helped her get a better job.

Once you have identified the traits/skills/characteristics that make you unique, write them down in the form of a memo, report, or book—if that is the space you need. You have to write it down for two reasons.

1. No one can see what is inside of you.

2. No one will spend forty hours to sit next to you and listen to your great ideas.

That's why you have to show them. Create a portfolio of past projects to present during a job interview; bring examples of your work, if possible. Be very specific about what you've done instead of using worn-out words like "energetic," "competent," and "proficient." Learn how to tell stories about yourself and your accomplishments. Sell yourself!

It Is All About Creating an Innovative Résumé

There is nothing wrong with a traditional résumé. But it probably doesn't truly capture who you are. If you want the opportunity to do your best work, you need to show potential employers how creative and special you really are. The first way to do that is to wow them with your résumé. Keep in mind that this résumé is every bit as important to you as it is to potential employers.

The text and exercises of this book are for you to discover yourself. By creating your art of war résumé, the person you're *really* selling yourself to . . . is you.

REFLECTION

Start to build your unique and powerful résumé . . . now!

Write down those ideas inside your heart that have been simmering for some time—your vision, aspirations, executions—that no one but you has yet seen.

_____

_____

_____

_____

_____

_____

_____

The Five Essentials for Victory

There are five ways to victory:

- She who knows when to fight and when not to fight, wins.

- She who knows when to use many or few troops, wins.

- She who obtains the wholehearted support of her troops, wins.

- She who is well prepared to seize favorable opportunities, wins.

- She who can free herself from interference from superiors, wins.

These five essentials are the Tao to victory.

When Sun Tzu had the unquestionable support of the Wu king, he had the five essentials under his control. He could make decisions freely. And just as he predicted in the quote, his armies won the battles they fought.

However, after the old king died and his son became king, Sun Tzu faded away.

You cannot always control all the requirements for victory—in other words, the whims of your employers, the direction of your organization, or even the state of your industry or the economy as a whole. Not even Master Sun could control outside factors such as the environment, the weather, the political climate. But you need to try to control as many as you can.

Delving Deeper

Let's take these five points apart using a hypothetical example to better understand how they can affect our everyday work lives.

Janet, a young businesswoman, wrote a proposal outlining her vision to create an affordable day spa for working women. Not only would the prices be lower, but the facials and massages would not last as long as the ones at spas catering to nonworking women who have all day to pamper themselves.

The CEO of Janet's firm, Robert, liked the proposal and suggested that she work with an outside architect to help turn her vision into reality. Janet thought working with others to refine her vision wouldn't be a problem.

She was wrong.

She hired John, an architect whom her firm had worked with in the past. Janet and John were almost done designing the new facility when Robert said he wanted to be more involved in the project.

It took only one brief conversation for it to become clear that Robert had a totally different vision about the spa. As Janet tried to incorporate everyone's vision into one cohesive plan, her original idea was lost in the shuffle.

Let's look at where Janet went wrong. She got her project off to a great start by following the fourth essential—in other words, by seizing upon a favorable opportunity: the need for a spa that would reach an underserved market of working women. But she violated Sun Tzu's second "essential" when it comes to insuring victory: She did not know—or in this case, did not have sufficient control over—the right number of troops to use. As Janet put it: "There were too many cooks in the kitchen."

I bet you can relate to Janet's story. When there are too many people involved in a project, their good intentions create more confusion than results. But you won't always have control of how many people should get involved in your project, so if you find yourself in Janet's position, what should you do? Remember the first "essential": "She who knows when to fight and when not to fight, wins."

Since Janet is already under contract to her company, fighting is not an option. She must do as her boss says, even though she might have to shoulder the blame if the spa fails. The only thing she can do here is go along with the agreed-on vision and hope for the best, making sure she does not make the same mistake in the future.

Once again, she displayed her mastery of the fourth "essential," "she who is well prepared to seize favorable opportunities, wins."

Recognizing that she wouldn't have final say, Janet tried to incorporate the best of everyone's thinking into her design, expanding her vision and hoping there would be a better result the next time.

That brings us to the importance of the last essential: "She who can free herself from interference from superiors, wins."

Next time, if possible, Janet needs to fight hard at the onset of a project to gain final approval over the design. She will need her boss to agree to this before the work begins. If she can't gain this approval, she needs to rethink whether she wants to be involved.

How can you obtain the clout you need to ensure that your vision becomes a reality? Keep the third "essential" in mind: *She who obtains the wholehearted support of her troops, wins.*

In Janet's case, her company wants the spa to be a financial success. If she can convince them that her plan has the chance to make that happen, she could get the support she needs.

Janet knows the timing to build this unique affordable spa for working women is right. The research she has done confirms a market is there. Because sometimes opportunity, indeed, does not knock twice, she can't waste time fighting with Robert. She needs to act swiftly and decisively to fold the best of Robert's and John's ideas into her initial vision.

The Essentials

You might not always have control over the five essentials, as Sun Tzu did initially, but if you can master a couple of them, then victory is attainable.

EXAMPLE

Long-term Objective: Published Author

Plan of action: It won't do you any good to send your manuscript to your ten favorite authors begging for their help. What's in it for them? If you really want help, first write to an author you admire and explain that you will help promote his or her book in your town by contacting bookstores, local associations, community chambers of commerce, local businesses, and lead a discussion group or start a readers club focusing on his or her book. Keep the author posted regarding your dynamic results. Then you have earned the trust and appreciation of that author. You're already one step ahead of the game and gotten one foot in the door of that industry.

Long-term objective: _____

_____

Plan of action: _____

_____

_____

_____

CHAPTER 4

Disposition
Win First, Then Fight

This chapter of Sun Tzu's can be summed up in one word: *xing*, which means "shape." Specifically, the term refers to both mental and physical dispositions needed for offensive and defensive battles. Both dispositions should be constantly present in our everyday lives.

The first part of this chapter—win before you fight—is about mental disposition, and it is not as strange as it might first sound. If you have taken every possible step to ensure victory before the battle begins, if you have covered every option and eliminated every conceivable chance of being defeated, then victory is assured—even before the first shot is fired.

When discussing how to win before fighting, Master Sun gave, in the opening of his Chapter 4, the steps to victory:

- Create conditions that your enemy cannot overcome.

- Wait for the right opportunity (the right timing) before you begin the battle, so that you can put your opponent at the biggest disadvantage possible.

- You are the one who decides whether the battle is worth fighting. If you are not certain of victory, don't fight.

- Victory is ultimately created by your opponent. He will do certain things that guarantee his defeat—and your victory. Take advantage of them.

- You can create both offensive and defensive strategies that are insurmountable.

Notice what Master Sun is saying. In the West, most strategy books begin with the premise that you are the "master of your destiny," in charge of your victory. The assumption is that you must take proactive steps to achieve success.

Yet Sun is saying that victory is *not* in your control but rather the gift of your enemy—in other words, victory is assured when your enemy makes a mistake. Of course, it's up to you to pinpoint your enemy's weakness and exploit it. This is a much more realistic take on winning in a competitive business environment.

Consider the Super Bowl: a battle between the two best teams in football. Both teams are strong and usually pretty evenly matched, so initially there is no guarantee who will win. Yet invariably, the team that makes the fewest mistakes is the victor.

Let's look at some of the offensive and defensive moves that can ensure we won't lose—and just may help us win.

Win Before You Fight

Ancient warriors first place themselves in an invincible position, then wait for the opportunity to defeat their enemies.

This statement, which opens Chapter 4 of *Sun Tzu's Art of War,* is one of the most mysterious in the entire book. Everyone has attempted to make sense of it, but few have.

Still, that doesn't stop people from quoting it. It makes them sound tough and smart—even if they don't know what it means! And so in books, movies, and on television shows, right before the pivotal battle, you often hear some version of the statement.

On the surface, the statement seems to be telling us that the time to fight is after you have already won. But the comment really goes a lot deeper.

Master Sun is really saying that you need to know that every part of your battle plan—all strategies, tactics, and contingencies—are in place and certain to work well before the battle begins. Born in the midst of a civil war that lasted 550 years, Sun Tzu knew the only sure thing about a war, once it's begun, is that there are no sure things.

Preparation for any battle in the workplace includes anticipating everything that could possibly happen after your initial attack. That means having the ability to alter course once the battle is under way.

The reason you need that ability is simple: No matter how hard you work, no matter how much you prepare, you will encounter things that you didn't plan for once the fighting begins. You will have to adapt.

But how can you change on the spur of the moment? By tapping into a force that is inside you, one that comes to the fore when you are engaged in the battle. I'm talking about the genius and the talent within you.

Well-written business plans and brilliant marketing proposals look wonderful on paper, but as many CEOs will tell you, the problem with business plans is that they do not include the unexpected frictions that are sure to occur once they are put into motion. The battle plan will change as your opponents grow stronger. What will remain is *you*—your indomitable will, your resolve, your winning vision.

You need to be prepared mentally to achieve victory. The proper mind-set is a key component of achieving that invincibility.

Victory Appears in Your Mind First

Victorious soldiers win first, then seek battle; vanquished soldiers fight first, then seek victory.

Recently I got a letter from a young woman who sells insurance, explaining how difficult she found it to make a sale. But as I see it, she was fighting the wrong war. She thinks she is trying to win over potential customers. But the first battle is in her head. She must convince herself that she is going to make the sale before she ever tries to make it.

Once she gets in front of her prospects, she has to forget about her commission (remember, focusing only on monetary gain is in direct conflict with Tao) and instead focus on her potential client's well-being. Her aim should not be to win one sale at the time, but to create a winning mind-set that allows her to win again and again. The only way she can do that is by convincing herself that she is going to make the sale.

A winner experiences winning in her body, mind, and soul before she even goes to fight the battle. All saleswomen know, or should know, that you cannot begin talking to a customer *hoping* to make a sale. You have to have sold your customer in your mind before you can ever sell him or her in reality.

Whether that sale means convincing your superiors that your proposal is better than those of your colleagues or winning a new client or customer, you can't go into the fight saying "I hope I win." Instead, you must already have a picture in your head about what victory will look like. Only then can you start to work backward to determine how to make that victory come about.

The Marriage of Strategy and a Winner's Attitude

Somewhere along the line, business wisdom got split into two main categories.

The first approach is usually referred to as motivational. This kind of advice often is packed with cheerleading and a constant reminder to tell yourself "I can do it" when confronted with any business problem.

The other style deals solely with strategy, and the tone is generally dry and formula-driven.

When you read books or articles about either of these two subjects, it is as if they exist in a vacuum. That's nonsense. Clearly, we need to integrate strategy and motivation.

No matter what business strategies you know, if you do not have a winner's attitude or a winner's soul, all your strategies will be wasted.

That is why people say "There are paper generals and battle-field generals." A paper general hasn't a clue what to do out in the real world when faced with problems he or she hadn't planned for.

The battlefield general knows how to combine strategy with a winning attitude. She isn't afraid to fight and knows how to make things happen.

The Joy of Winning

How do you achieve a winning attitude? Simply wanting to win, obviously, does not make you a winner, but it is the necessary first step. Before you engage in any battle—in the boardroom or outside the office—you must discover if there are any psychological blocks standing between you and winning.

We all *think* we want to win, yet many love the joy of struggle far more than the joy of winning.

Brianne, a friend of mine, is a bright and hardworking entry-level saleswoman. She works in sales for a $5 billion private company that manufactures machines that produce computer chips. She said to me once, "I'm so tired. Doing my job is like pulling a stubborn cow uphill." Her company is succeeding yet her own sales are meager.

After we talked a bit, she realized that, as a child, she always won very easily. Because she felt guilty about always beating the other kids, she'd learned to downplay her accomplishments—and eventually started performing poorly on purpose to even the playing field. After examining her behavior, she began to realize she's started to enjoy the struggle with the rest of humanity just to prove she is a nice "normal" person. To her, it was more important to be liked than to be successful. I told her, "Be nice to yourself first. Let the rest of humanity take care of themselves."

After this, her work became much easier and her sales increased by 246 percent the following year. Recently she told me she'd given up her attachment to the struggle. "I've begun focusing on the winning. Now I feel so much peace. With a win-first mind-set, everything became easier."

Winning by Wearing Glass Slippers
or Combat Boots

The power to prevent our enemy from conquering us lies in
our hands. The opportunity for us to defeat the enemy is
provided by the enemy.

If applied to the modern working world, the quote above tells us
that women have the power to ensure our invincibility in our areas of expertise. But if we do not embrace that power, we provide an opportunity for our supposed "enemies" (men and the
glass ceiling) to step in and defeat us.

In other words, while we are in control of our own invulner-
ability, it is our enemy who has control over our vulnerability. As
long as we see the glass ceiling as an indestructible enemy, we
give up our ability to break through it. It is not the glass ceiling
that is mighty in and of itself—it is our belief that it will hold us
back that gives it power.

In this chapter, I urge you to stop seeing the glass ceiling as a
potential enemy that can render you vulnerable. Instead, I encourage you to make yourself invulnerable to thoughts that
you're being held back because you're a woman. How? By envi-
sioning yourself as the master of your *own* idea of success.

We could blame gender inequality solely on men, but doing
so would be inconsistent with Tao and we would be wrong.

Yes, men have contributed to the oppression of women, but
we must also shoulder some of the blame. Why? Because we lie
to ourselves. We have trained our minds to think of success in a
certain way—the *male* way; it's only about getting ahead, climb-
ing the corporate ladder, becoming CEO.

Many of us suppress contrary definitions of success—things
that have absolutely nothing to do with achieving a fancy corpo-

rate title—as "unacceptable" because we fear that by telling the truth about who we really are and what we really want, the world we have so carefully cultivated may come crashing down around us.

And so we go around unconsciously lying to ourselves and pursuing what we think we should instead of what is truly important to us.

That is no way to live your life.

If you dig down deep enough to discover who you are, what you want, and what is right for you, your honesty will guide you to your personal happiness.

And if many women are honest with themselves, they will admit that they don't want to be CEOs. Some just want a certain level of comfort and a decent paycheck; they want to be able to take care of their family, spend time with their friends, read good books, travel, wear sneakers and comfortable clothes, and create a nurturing environment for their loved ones.

Others want all this and more—a fulfilling career, but often one that does not overwhelm their lives.

But in both cases, these women are made to feel guilty for not having "enough ambition," and so they make excuses; blaming the "glass ceiling" is an easy one. It is easier to say "They just won't promote a woman" than it is to be honest and say "I really don't want the pressure and time commitment that comes with a top job."

Waiting for the White Knight

If you are unable to win, then defend.
If you can win, then attack.

Then there is the woman who wants to get promoted but wears glass slippers. She has the ambition, but she doesn't yet have the warrior spirit. She wants success but is unable to give up her "Cinderella attitude." Let me explain this phrase.

Deep inside many women, there is a small part that longs to be Cinderella, that is waiting for Prince Charming to come along and carry her off to a life of luxury and ease.

There is nothing wrong with that fantasy, especially considering that it's a story we've been told since we were little girls. However, you cannot climb the corporate ladder with glass slippers on; for that you need combat boots. It takes a warrior to climb the ladder.

Again, let me stress that there is nothing wrong with any choice you may make. You may want to put family first; you may want to balance—as best you can—family and career; or you may want to give everything you have in a quest to become CEO.

The problem is not with any of these choices. The point is, we need to choose: Do we want the comfy sneakers, the glass slippers, or the combat boots? Don't lie. Don't justify. Be proud of your choice.

It is easy enough to find the external villains. There is no question that men have discriminated against us. But the major force keeping us down is our confusion about what we want.

Before we can move forward as a gender, we should take a sober look at how we contribute to our own misery. Let's examine some of the factors that make us feel so unhappy.

Why Is It So Hard for Women to Find the Right "Shoes"?

1. *We place fantasies above reality.* The other day a (male) bank manager I know confided, "I would really like to promote capable females and nurture them, but I cannot find qualified candidates."

I looked around and saw why he was so frustrated. You could

tell from the way the women in his bank talked, acted, and dressed that they did not take their careers seriously. Even though they were working in a conservative banking environment, most dressed as if they were schoolkids going to a class.

Some wore long, flowery dresses, others miniskirts with lacy blouses. To these women, it was more important to be sexy, trendy young "chicks" than to dress like tomorrow's female executives.

Of course, this rule of appropriate dress is not used to discriminate against women. Men, too, won't be promoted in conservative work environments if they insist on wearing T-shirts and shorts.

> Everything—our clothes, our attitudes, our skills— shows what we think about our job. How can we expect to be promoted if we do not envision ourselves as worthy for advancement and express that attitude outwardly?

2. We lie to ourselves about what we want.

> Thus one may know how to win
> but be unable to execute victory.

It's perfectly fine to say "I work to support myself and help out my family." If that's your choice, you should be very proud of it. It is a noble motivation, one in line with Tao, universal righteousness. A mother wanting to make money to improve her family's standard of living is acting in a way that is consistent with Tao. It's right. It's appropriate.

If this is truly what you want, and you are doing it, you are a winner. It is the woman who says one thing—"I want to be

CEO"—and feels another—"I really don't want to work that hard"—who ends up miserable.

3. *We wear glass slippers with combat fatigues.* The most unhappy woman is the one caught between her dream of being Cinderella and doing what she must to gain recognition and advancement in the workplace. As a result, she ends up being ineffective in both worlds.

You have to throw away either the glass slippers or the combat fatigues.

If you choose to keep the combat fatigues, wear the boots, too. The glass slippers go with the ball gown.

Whatever you decide, commit to it and have fun.

4. *We buy in to the myth of the glass ceiling.* For the real warrior who wishes to ascend, it is not the glass ceiling but the *myth* of the glass ceiling that often stops her.

It would be misguided to deny the existence of the glass ceiling, but worrying about it does you no good. Focus on what will benefit you, instead of concentrating on that which will bring you down.

In a business dominated by men, the late Dawn Steel was the first woman to become president of a major movie studio—Columbia Pictures. When asked about the glass ceiling, she replied that she could not see it. It did not exist for her. Now, certainly it was there; otherwise she would not have been an exception. But she chose not to see it.

Recently I was invited by Hélène Larivée, the general manager of Cirque du Soleil, to see a performance given by the troupe that is by far the most artistic and inspiring circus on earth.

I told Hélène I'd always thought of the circus as a macho, male-dominated world. I asked her to tell me the single most effective element that has contributed to her success in this environment.

Hélène, a delicate-looking woman who stands just a little

over five feet, replied, "I have always worked with men and I never felt that I was different from them."

Because Hélène presents herself as a powerful, proficient businesswoman, men see her this way too.

The majority of men in a position to promote women are not stupid; they know it is to their advantage to work with capable individuals regardless of their gender.

> Successful women worldwide have one thing in common: They don't see the glass ceiling.

5. We lack a powerful spirit.

> When lacking strength, defend.
> When full of strength, attack.

Power comes from our spirit, and without it, we are weak. We can enhance our outward appearance by dressing and speaking well, but we can't fake spirit.

Let me give you two examples. I once attended a party where I was introduced to a woman who worked as a trainer for the phone company. This woman was constantly taking classes to better herself; she dressed and talked like a corporate professional. And yet she didn't believe she was getting promoted as fast as she should.

As I began to talk to her, I kept feeling something was missing. Eventually I figured it out. Susan is from Georgia and, as a southern woman, she was brought up to be charming and feminine. She'd never learned to be assertive, especially around men.

Deep down she believed that the "Type A" behavior required to succeed at work is unfeminine and therefore inappropriate. No wonder her bosses concluded that she was not enough of a go-getter to be promoted. Susan will have to either overcome her upbringing or become resigned to doing work that doesn't challenge her. All that dressing for success, mastery of corporate vocabulary, and charm will never overcome the feeling of powerlessness in her soul.

In contrast, when I first met Datuk Seri Rafidah, the Malaysian minister of international trade, I thought the prime minister had been out of his mind to appoint her to such a high position. She was dressed in a metallic, rainbow-colored floor-length Malay dress. Her arms, neck, and ears were decorated with gold ornaments, and her eyes were painted bright blue, certainly not the way we in the West are taught a leader should look. However, as soon as she opened her mouth, I discovered her spirit was as bright and luminous as her style.

Walking the walk and talking the talk can get you so far, but it's the spirit behind your actions, words, and appearance that announces your inner state.

Solutions to Sexual Discrimination

If you are convinced that you are not getting ahead because of your gender, then you should:

1. Find people whose judgment you trust and ask them what the problem is. In one of my workshops, a woman complained that she hadn't been promoted because of sexual discrimination. I brought her onstage and asked her to role-play various interactions she had at work. The entire audience could see that she needed to work on her confidence, body language, and clarity in communication. The problem wasn't discrimination. It was her.

2. If you really are being discriminated against and don't like your job, then start looking for another one.

3. If you like your job and don't want to quit, then work even harder. By doing so, a couple of things can happen. If you are really superior, you may stand a better chance of being promoted because it will be in your boss's best interest to utilize you in a more effective way. Of course, you may find yourself passed over for key projects and promotions because your boss is afraid you will take over his or her job. In this case, the universe has made the decision for you: It is time for you to move on to a better job elsewhere.

It Is All About Combat Boots and Glass Slippers

To secure ourselves against defeat lies in our own doing;
the victory is provided by the enemy.

As Sun Tzu correctly points out, you may not have total control over whether you succeed or not. Success depends in part on the circumstances you face.

However, you can keep yourself from being defeated. There are two common reasons we often lose.

First, we wear the wrong shoes for the wrong occasion. In the workplace, combat boots (and not glass slippers) are required.

Second, we give ourselves excuses to fail. As Master Sun says, securing yourself against defeat depends on your own effort. In other words, you can't blame anyone else if things don't work out. Among other things, from this moment on we can dismiss the "glass ceiling" as an excuse forever.

We are winners when we are content with our work and our position, whether it is prestigious or humble in the eyes of the masses. How others view you doesn't matter. If you are happy with who you are, you are a winner.

The world is large enough to hold dreams of different sizes

and colors. No one dream is inherently better than the others. It does not matter if you prefer to wear glass slippers or combat boots. As long as you are truthful with yourself, and your actions are in line with Tao, there will always be a happy future waiting for you.

REFLECTION

What are the most important goals in your life? Rate the following with 1 being most important and 10 being least important.

_____ Getting promoted

_____ Starting my own business

_____ Spending time with my family

_____ Traveling

_____ Cooking

_____ Making money

_____ _____

_____ _____

_____ _____

_____ _____

CHAPTER 5

Momentum
Use Timing
to Generate Momentum

S un Tzu had a one-word title for the fifth chapter of his *Art of War*: *shi*, which means "momentum."

He uses the word as we do today—as a synonym for the energy or drive to propel something—and as you will see in this chapter, the key to creating momentum is to take advantage of an area where you can clearly dominate your opponent.

Master Sun believed that momentum can be gained by managing differently, thinking differently, acting differently (specifically in a way that will confuse your opponents), and, perhaps most intriguingly, by tapping into the forces that are all around you—especially the universal timing that will allow you to create favorable momentum.

5.1

The Twenty-first Century, the Woman's Century

The rushing water generates tremendous momentum, enough to float giant stones.

The flying eagle is able to destroy its prey due to its precise coordination of distance and time.

A skillful warrior marches her troops into battle by stirring up an overwhelming force of momentum.

Exactly what is the difference between universal timing, which is beyond our control, and personal timing, which we can influence?

In order to answer this question, we have to step back to view our lives as Sun Tzu did.

There are powerful natural forces in the universe. Rushing water is certainly one of them, and as Master Sun noted, this can either be a blessing—the force can be enough to turn a water-wheel that powers a mill—or a curse—if it is not channeled properly, the same surging water can wipe out a town.

But I don't think Sun was being literal when he spoke of the natural forces such as rushing water and soaring eagles. As the last part of the quote—where he refers to stirring up the troops—shows, he was also speaking metaphorically.

For example, in the same quote, we could replace the "rushing water" with "our own (ever-rushing) thoughts." If we do, then we can think of universal timing as an idea whose time has come.

When you have that universal timing on your side, you are unstoppable. And that is what is happening to women in this new millennium—we are becoming an unstoppable force. We are moving from the Industrial Revolution to the Information Revolution, from the Man's Century to the Woman's Century. This is not just a slogan or rallying cry. We can easily turn it into reality.

Riding the Universal Timing

Tao supports the equality of Yin and Yang. Our world was created with equality in mind. Women must see through the myths of male superiority. In the natural course of human evolution, the power of Yin (the feminine) will swell and expand unstoppably like the waxing of the moon. What was held back and humbled will rise high and be glorified.

This is the principle of Tao and the universal righteousness. Anything against Tao will seek its own destruction or correction.

Given women's nature, this new era will most likely be a more balanced and compassionate chapter in humanity's "herstory." Simply by coming to power, women will break from the male tradition of repeating history. Rather, they will re-create it. Just as the human race re-creates itself through a woman's body and improves as it evolves, so will humanity evolve when Yin and Yang are balanced.

And that transformation is already under way, as women worldwide tap into the forces that will make the twenty-first century our time. You see it everywhere.

- In 2006, *CFO* magazine reported that there were 35 female CFOs in the Fortune 500. This is a 350 percent gain from 1995, the first year the magazine conducted the survey, when only 10 women held the title.

- According to the National Women's Business Council, twenty-five years ago women owned about 10 percent of

U.S. businesses. Today, women have majority ownership in 48 percent of the nation's privately held businesses.

- Ninety percent of U.S. banking companies (compared with only 78 percent of foreign companies) have at least one woman director, according to a 2005 study by Corporate Woman Directors International.

- In August 2006, Indra Nooyi was named CEO of Pepsi Co., becoming the first female CEO in the company's history, and the 11th female CEO in the Fortune 500.

- According to a study by Catalyst, a nonprofit research and advisory organization working to advance women in business and the professions, in 2004, Fortune 500 companies with the highest percentages of women corporate officers yielded, on average, a 35.1 percent higher return on equity and 34.0 percent higher total return to shareholders than those with the lowest percentages of women corporate officers.

By all accounts, things are getting much better. But there is always room for improvement. "America needs to accelerate the rate by which more women lead Fortune 500 companies and participate in their boardrooms if we are to hold on to our global market dominance," says Linda K. Bolliger, founder and CEO, Boardroom Bound, whose program prepares and promotes diversity in the corporate boardroom. "The twenty-first century calls for consensus building in order for institutions to survive."

Two More Trends in Our Favor

The twenty-first century is commonly spoken of as the Pacific Century, because the Pacific region is, and will be, the leading area of growth worldwide. Along with the rise of Pacific economic power, we will also witness an increased influx of Pacific cultural values, which tend more toward the intangible and intuitive than western values.

In my mind, the dominant themes of western culture—being direct, acting rationally and logically, and saying what's on your mind—are masculine qualities. The Pacific or Asian qualities are distinctly feminine—intuitive, subtle. Pacific culture recognizes a full spectrum of grays and accepts that life is filled with ambiguities and paradox.

Feminine qualities such as empathy, intuition, love, and accommodation weren't valued—to be blunt, they were denigrated—during the masculine-dominated industrial era.

Now, as we move deeper into the Information Age, muscle power is no longer the dominant force driving society; brainpower is. The innate female abilities to discern fine shades of meaning and negotiate the unknown will turn out to be the essential competitive tools during this century.

> The time has come for the Woman's Century.

The combination of the Information Age and the Pacific Century will cause a great explosion in our awareness of feminine energy. Masculine strength will give way to the subtler intuitive faculties that are capable of reaching and touching beyond the norm. Gradually, the twenty-first century will become dominated by this feminine energy. We already have women running Fortune 100 companies. I feel confident that during the twenty-first century, there will be a female U.S. president.

Among the five elements (gold, wood, water, fire, earth) there is no eternal conqueror.

The four seasons rotate and make way for each other, just as daylight has long and short, and the moon has waxing and waning.

The fact that men have had political and economic power for the past few millennia is a function of Tien, universal timing. But these same forces that put men in the ascendancy will uplift women in the twenty-first century.

However, this does not mean everything will be easy; while heaven does her part, we have to do ours. And it is up to every individual woman to take full advantage of this blessed timing.

5.2

Six Steps to Improve Your Personal Timing

A proficient warrior seeks victory
by employing opportune timing.

Timing really *is* everything. You cannot sell people something when they don't want it; rather, your products must answer an unconscious longing within them. When they see it, they will realize they have been waiting for it. The timing is right.

If your product or service is ahead of the general public's taste, sales will lag. If it hits the market too late, you miss the trend. In either case, the timing wasn't right.

> Great timing (Tien) is born out of the synchronicity between the surfacing of unconscious collective desires and the readiness of the perfect ideas/products/people to meet those desires.

In the last chapter I discussed ways that you could tap into universal timing. The obvious follow-up question is: Is there a way I can improve my personal timing?

I think there is. In fact, I think there are six things you can do to improve your timing and by doing so increase your chances of success.

How We Can Improve Our Timing

1. Notice the signals of timing hidden all around. An idea whose time has almost come gives subtle—but unmistakable—hints, often even leaving behind a physical trail of its presence.

Take the fashion business, for example. Most people believe that designers dictate what we will wear—that each "look" springs solely out of their imaginations.

The designers themselves don't think that is the case. During an interview, Donna Karan was asked how she determined what to design for the next season.

Her answer was disarmingly simple. She explained that she paid attention to the signals, large and small, all around her. Certain colors or designs would appear and reappear over and over on the street, in the subway, or on television. These signals let her know what was going on in the mind of the masses. She used these signs as a guide to make sure that she was on the right track with what she was designing.

Every woman can relate to this. At one time or another, we

each have used this "nonscientific" commonsense process to help us make decisions about when, how, and whether to proceed with certain projects.

2. *Be in tune with the timing of potential partners.*

The flying eagle is able to destroy its prey due to its precise coordination of distance and time.

This is something Sun Tzu understood well. He wrote:

The skillful warrior, during battle, avoids the enemy's high-spirited moments and attacks when the enemy is anxious.

Here's a simple example. People in the seminar business know that timing—scheduling, in their case—is critical to a seminar's success. If their companies pay the seminar fee, attendees prefer that the seminar be held during the business week. If they are paying for the seminar themselves, they want it to be held on a weekend. And, of course, seminar planners try not to hold events between Thanksgiving and New Year's, when people are dealing with the stress and the complications of the holidays.

If you are making a sales call or presenting a business proposal, it is best to avoid your customers' resistive periods. Each customer has at least one, but it is up to you to learn when it is. For some, it could be Monday morning; for others, Friday afternoon.

I know a magazine publisher whose most mellow time is after five-thirty, when all the employees have left and the office chaos has settled down. This is the best time to reach him. (It also helps that by five-thirty, his assistant has gone home for the day and he answers his own phone.)

3. Be aware of the relationship between your objective and your timing.

> The good warrior's staging of an attack is like the bending of the crossbow full of momentum and potential.
>
> When she releases the trigger, the arrow flies with a precise calculation combining distance, timing, and target. Not too early, not too late.

Odds are your climb to the top will take longer—often a lot longer—than you would like. You will not become CEO during your second week as an administrative assistant.

When you are not aware of how long it will take to achieve your objective, you're like a farmer constantly pulling crops up by the root to see how fast they are growing. You need a realistic understanding of how long it will take to achieve your objective.

There are no hard-and-fast rules here. Timing doesn't always mean being first to market. Diet Coke didn't create the first no-calorie soft drink market. Dell didn't invent the personal computer. Southwest Airlines wasn't the first regional airline.

There are times when you might want your competitor to launch her product first, paying for the high cost of educating consumers, distributors, and retailers about what the new innovation is all about. And then, only when the market is ready, do you come swooping in.

You have to determine where your strengths lie. If it is in research and development, then you do want to be first to market. If you are best at controlling costs—and therefore can be the low-cost supplier—then you want to follow the leaders and undercut their prices. The point is to align your objective with timing.

4. Use your intuition to improve your timing. A prominent publisher once told me, "I stick my finger up and feel what the air is telling me about which book to buy." I don't think she was joking.

Timing is closely associated with intuition, that gut feeling that you cannot necessarily explain but that invariably leads you to the right decision. If we can tap our intuition, it can certainly help us detect the "rightness" of our timing.

People who are sensitive, empathic, and loving and who give freely tend to be more naturally intuitive.

You can take some simple steps to sharpen your intuition:

a. Intuition is like a muscle; the more you use it, the better it will develop. Whenever possible, before trying to "figure out" the right answer to a problem you're facing, try to *sense* what to do.

   Start small. Before you open your mailbox, try to "feel" what's inside the box. Is the box very full or rather empty? What does it look like—is it full of a lot of magazines and junk mail, or only a couple of letters?

b. When you "guessed" correctly, note your state of mind. Odds are you were calm. We generally call this the "gut feeling," and far too many of us ignore it—often, as we realize later, to our detriment.

   There is a reason that the first sentence of Dr. Benjamin Spock's *Baby and Child Care*, the child-rearing bible, is "You know more than you think you do."

   In *The Power of Intuition* (Doubleday/Currency), Gary Klein, a psychologist and noted researcher, very carefully and methodically lays out a convincing case that can be boiled down to this: Trust your gut.

   Yes, skills, training, and education are helpful, but don't underestimate the power of intuition.

   "I define intuition as the way we translate our experience into action," writes Klein, who heads his own consulting firm. "Our experience lets us recognize what is going on (making judgments) and how to react (making decisions.) Because our experience enables us to recognize what to do . . . we don't deliberately have to think through issues to arrive at good decisions [quickly]."

c. Practice meditation to calm your mind down so you can be a sharp radio receiver, someone who takes in images without unwanted mental static. You'll be amazed at what you're able to see. There are many different types of meditation that you can explore, but a good way to start is simply by sitting quietly and focusing on your breath. You may find it helpful to look at a vast space, such as the ocean, desert, or sky. There are also activities and games that can help you improve your focus: golf and knitting are two examples. Even sitting in a rocking chair can help calm the mind.

5. Back up your intuition with data and planning. Sun Tzu believed that there are only three approaches to planning, and he explained the consequences of each:

a. Meticulous planning. Before engaging in battle, you have already won the war.

b. Careless planning. Before engaging in battle, you may have already lost the war.

c. No planning. Your defeat is certain.

In other words, planning is the key to success. Until you are absolutely certain of your instincts, you should plan on gathering solid data to back up your intuition. By tapping into your gut feeling (intuition) you can narrow down the 360 degrees of possibilities to a specific direction. Once you set your direction, then gather data to prove or disprove the workability of your gut feelings.

Don't become your own worst enemy.
Use your instincts to determine when the time is
right to set your plans in motion.

6. *Use common sense.* As Master Sun put it, "There is a proper season and time for utilizing fire to attack the enemy." If the wind is blowing toward you, for example, you would not set fire to the enemy camp.

Always check which way the wind is blowing before you attempt to introduce a new idea at work.

Thinking About Ways to Improve Your Personal Timing

A skillful warrior marches her troops into battle by stirring
up an overwhelming force of momentum.

You can improve your personal timing by tapping into your personal intuition and by doing your homework, but unless your intentions are in line with Tao, your timing will always be off.

We may not be able to control timing, but we can improve it by supplementing our intuition with common sense and experience and then following up by executing our plans in an ethical (and timely) manner.

By incorporating Tao into our day-to-day lives, we will naturally improve our timing. Where there is timing, there is momentum, and with momentum on your side, you'll find it much easier to achieve your goals.

CHAPTER 6

Real and Unreal
Illusion Is the Other Side of Reality

The title of Sun Tzu's sixth chapter is composed of two words, *si* and *xu*. *Xu* means "unreal," "empty," "illusive." *Si* means "real," "solid," "full." In the philosophy of the Tao, which Master Sun studied and followed, what appears to be real may be unreal, what looks full may really be empty, what seems to be weak is actually strong.

As Lao Tzu, the greatest of the Tao's philosophers, said, "In this universe, we can see beauty as beauty because of its contrast with ugliness." Beauty and ugliness are two sides of the same coin. Tao's philosophy sees the whole universe as a deceptive illusion. The world is not real. It is but the dream of the divine, yet it appears real to the human. In Chapter 6, Sun Tzu explores this philosophical point.

The most important message of this chapter may sound counterintuitive, but it's true: Illusions should play a central role in the reality you create.

Unfortunately, this is a lesson that women have learned the hard way. Throughout history women have been represented in a false and misleading way. We are not weak, we are not overly emotional, we are not incapable of leading—but for thousands of years, that's exactly how we've been perceived. Somewhere along the line, the illusion became reality, and the reality that we are just as strong and capable as men was forgotten.

Fortunately, times have changed. Today we can use the illusion of our weakness and fragility to our advantage, by causing our competitors and enemies to underestimate us. As this chapter will reveal, in a battle, the truth is less important than what your opponents believe to be true.

I am not talking about lying. (I personally am a terrible liar and don't believe that it is ever a good business practice.) But you can let people believe what they want to believe, especially if they believe you are less capable than you truly are.

6.1

A Womanhood Makeover

Be without form.

According to Taoist philosophy, what you can see—that which has form—is not real. What you cannot see—the formless—is the reality of the universe. Think about atomic particles; we cannot see them, yet they make up the foundation of everything we and our world are made of. According to this logic, the "truths about women" that have held up in the past can be considered unreal. It is now up to us to "repackage" ourselves.

As we all know, a product needs to be packaged in such a way that people can tell at a glance exactly what it is. Is it a luxury car or an affordable vehicle? A place to grab a quick bite or a fine-dining experience? A "date movie" or one that's "just for the guys"? Invariably, we can answer those questions in a second or two, just based on how the product is advertised and marketed.

We can also think of womanhood as a "product." Of course, it is probably the most deceptively mislabeled and misrepresented product in human history. We have been marketed as inferior and unholy and represented by every demeaning symbol mankind—and I chose that word deliberately—could dream up.

First, let me give you one quick example that proves the point (as if it needs proving). Then I'll explain how we can change our image.

The Myth of the Lone Fireman

When faced with a proficient general, the opponent does not know where to place her defense. When facing a general who is skilled in defense, she doesn't know how to attack.

Many people believe that women are not suited to be professional firefighters. "Even I—someone who thinks women can do almost anything as well as a man—draw the line at firefighting," I once told a retired New York City fireman after one of my speeches. "If I were trapped in a burning building, I would be very disappointed to see a female firefighter coming to my rescue. I would much prefer a great, hulking fireman."

The firefighter told me I had been taken in by the Hollywood image of one muscular man rushing into a burning building in order to save the helpless woman, cowering in the corner.

"There is almost no way a single person can rescue anyone from a burning building," he said. "Because each of us is loaded down with so much heavy equipment, we always work in teams. Whenever firefighters save someone," he continued, "it is a team effort."

How can women correct this misconception—as well as all the other misconceptions about men and women?

The answer: by selling the world a new image of womanhood.

We have to constantly present contrary images—not only of the female firefighter, but also of the female leader, the female scientist, the female athlete. It's time to embrace all the aspects of what it means to be a woman. Of course, you may find some of the following ideas apply to you more than others. The point is, every woman has different strengths that we can capitalize on.

Eight Ways to "Repackage" Womankind

1. Women are creators of beauty. Without women, the world would resemble a bachelor pad—smelly, dirty, and messy. Legend has it that when President Kennedy was a senator, before he married Jackie, his apartment in Washington was frequently knee-high in trash. Here was a man viewed as an elegant icon of style who couldn't even tidy up his apartment.

We women need to repackage ourselves as the representatives of beauty, order, and cleanliness here on earth. The world needs a feminine touch.

2. Women are the keepers of the light of humanity. With a few exceptions, since ancient times, men have been occupied with battles and wars, while women have minded the family and the home, providing the consistency necessary for humanity to continue. Of course, this is changing as women enter the workforce, politics, the sciences, and the military in ever-growing numbers, but as we move forward, we must not forget where we came from—and how our previous roles have made us even better equipped as businesspeople than our male counterparts. The light of humanity is expressed through woman's love, caring, and nurturing. Now, in the twenty-first century, the Woman's Century, these positive qualities are ever more important in the business world as we move from a vicious cutthroat era to one of cooperation.

Without harmony, love, beauty, and happiness, there would be no humanity to speak of. By ensuring these qualities, women keep the light of humanity burning brightly. Take Judy George, the creator of one of the world's leading furniture stores, Domain. George has made it her business to create a store that not only sells top-quality home furnishings but that also makes customers feel, well, at home. On her Web site, she states:

> *Domain isn't just about selling furniture, it's about fulfilling dreams. . . . For a long time, I had a vision of what a furniture store should look and feel like. So, I conducted extensive research and interviewed consumers all over the country about what they really wanted in a furniture store. They told me they loved their homes, but hated buying furniture. They were frustrated and afraid of making mistakes and large financial commitments. Long delivery times and "hard sell" salespeople discouraged them.*

George teamed this knowledge with her vision, and Domain was born. By following a few simple rules she created herself, including "Get support from those you love" and "Don't hide your feelings," George has created a furniture store that many people find as comfortable as their own homes.

3. *Women don't give up.* In business, the individual's inner toughness and the ability to endure the unendurable is essential for long-term success. (We are the tougher of the two genders. Women can endure much more pain than men; after all, we are the ones charged with the world's most painful job—child delivery. Most men would probably give up halfway!) You need to

call on that power of perseverance when things are not going your way.

Recently I was in Lowe's, the home building chain store, trying to find the right tile for my house. I found one box of the pattern I liked on the shelf, but there weren't enough tiles to cover the area I needed. So I asked three salesmen if they could find me more. All three gave me the same answer: Whatever is there, is there. Then I found a saleswoman named Adriana Pittaluga. After I told her what I was looking for, she climbed twenty feet up a big ladder and searched behind other boxes until she found one more box for me. Then she found another Lowe's store that had more and asked them to save them for me. When I thanked her, she answered quite profoundly, "Women just don't give up."

4. *Women are more sensible than men.* Common sense is the most important business tool when making the decisions that guide our everyday actions. Let's stay with the baby theme for a minute. A woman carries her baby for nine months with loving tenderness. She cares for herself and for her unborn. She changes her lifestyle—she eats better and gets more sleep—and deprives herself of numerous pleasures, such as wine, during her pregnancy.

But the deprivation doesn't end with pregnancy or the way we care for our families. The preservation and regeneration of humanity is anchored in a woman's practicality and extends to our everyday business and personal life.

5. *Women are intuitive.* As you know, the effectiveness of *Sun Tzu's Art of War* is closely tied to the individual's intuitiveness. Women are naturally intuitive. The skills that once ensured the survival of our infant babies can be applied to countless areas of our lives.

I always tell my male executive clients that when they are in doubt about any decision, they should either trust their feelings or ask their wife's advice. Women's innate intuition enhances our ability to master strategic thinking naturally.

6. *Women are the guardians of Mother Earth.* There are three essential forces at work in the universe: destruction, creation, and sustaining power. Men have thus far shown their immense talent for destruction. Together, men and women create new life. But it has always been up to women to sustain and nurture life in all forms. Women put forth the necessary mental and physical energy to sustain our earthly environment. Now we will use this same power to sustain our economic environment.

There may be no better example of this than Dame Anita Roddick, founder of The Body Shop, which now has two thousand stores serving some 80 million customers worldwide.

"Businesses have the power to do good," said Roddick. "We use our stores and our products to help communicate human rights and environmental issues. For me, campaigning and good business is also about putting forward solutions, not just opposing destructive practices."

According to its Web site, The Body Shop launched its Community Trade Programme in the late 1980s when Roddick began establishing trading relationships with suppliers from disadvantaged communities around the globe. Now, with thirty-five supplier partners from twenty-three countries, The Body Shop remains committed to using trade as a way to make a positive influence on the world.

7. *Women are strong.* In 1995 David Koch, an industrial billionaire and America's Cup winner, assembled the first all-women crew to ever compete in the America's Cup, the most prestigious sailing race. Everybody thought he was crazy! His friends said things like, Women are not strong enough, are not skilled enough as sailors, and are not smart enough to compete; why waste your money? The old guard in the yacht clubs just laughed and ridiculed his all-women team.

It finished third.

According to David, "If we had not made some fundamental mistakes about strategy, mistakes that had nothing to do with gender, these women possibly could have won. These women were incredibly strong. After training for about a year, they became so strong that none of the men on the other teams would dare mess with them physically."

It's time to stop thinking about strength in purely masculine terms. In a number of sports—open-water swimming, extreme marathons, and gymnastics, to name a few—women consistently outperform men because our bodies are naturally more flexible and durable. But that is not enough; we need to fight to change the very definition of "strength," which, until now, has been seen as a mostly masculine characteristic.

8. *Women are competitive.* Many believe that because women are by nature more compassionate and sensitive, we are not competitive. But that is not true.

> Just because women are sensitive and empathetic does not mean that we don't enjoy the thrill of competition.

The problem isn't that we aren't competitive; the problem is that, until recently, we have not been *allowed* to compete. We have no record of when the first women started to work, but there's no denying that up until the last few decades, next to no women held any kind of power in corporate life.

And there's no denying that, to this day, we're still playing catch-up. For example, even classical music—a field that many might not instantly view as a boys' club—is embarrassingly male dominated. According to *Time* magazine, until the middle of the twentieth century, "it was rare for orchestras to hire female instrumentalists, let alone female conductors. The Vienna Philharmonic was all male until 1997, when under the pressure of popular opinion it finally hired a female harpist. Among the top

75 symphony orchestras in the U.S., there are still only three female conductors."

Luckily, Marin Alsop didn't let that fact deter her. Recently appointed to conduct the Baltimore Symphony Orchestra, Alsop realizes that the time has never been better for women to step to the front of the stage. As the first woman to head a major orchestra, you can bet Alsop faced some fierce competition to get there—and by doing so she's also helped to break down our stereotypes. "There's this whole archetypal image of what a conductor is, this inaccessible person with an accent and an ascot," said Alsop in *Time*. "This is the age of collaboration rather than autocracy."

In other words, now is the right time for the Woman's Century—the collaborative century.

A Media Makeover?

Water finds its course according to the shape of the ground. The warrior achieves victory by devising strategies according to the conditions she is facing.

At a press conference in Singapore, Datuk Seri Rafidah Aziz, the Malaysian minister of international trade, was asked recently, "How can you juggle the responsibilities of your demanding work and your family duties?"

Her matter-of-fact reply?

"Why don't you ask Lee Kuan Yew [the founding father of Singapore, the past prime minister, and still the most powerful man in the city] how he juggles his office duties and his duty of being a father to his children and husband to his wife? Your question does not deserve an answer."

And with that, Aziz walked out, ending the press conference.

Actress Geena Davis had a similar experience when she appeared on CNN to promote See Jane, a company she founded that seeks to increase the number of female characters in children's programming. According to Page Rockwell, writing on *Salon's* Broadsheet blog, when Davis tried to talk about her work with See Jane, CNN host Kara Phillips steered the conversation to Davis's "amazing husband." As Rockwell dryly notes, "Maybe interviews with women are required to include mention of amazing husbands and beautiful children along with professional accomplishments. But it's a bummer that she [Davis] has to talk about her personal life instead of her media watchdog group in an interview that's ostensibly about her media watchdog group."

When a woman is able to balance a successful career with a happy family life, she *should* be applauded—but not at the risk of overshadowing her other accomplishments. This is a challenge that the media needs to address.

There's a simple solution to this kind of inequity in reporting. Before asking any woman about how she's able to balance her career with her family, reporters need to ask themselves: "If she were a man, would I be asking him this?"

6.2

Your Personal Makeover: Let Your Style Support Your Career

Water shapes its current from the lie of the land.
The warrior shapes his victory from the dynamic of the enemy.

Your first line of defense and offense is your style of dress. Of course, we need look no further than at the traditional business suit to recall that the style of dress for business was originally designed for men, by men. Women marched into men's domain as intruders, camouflaging ourselves in clothes that men long ago decided were appropriate for business. As time passed, we added our touch and creatively took the boring business suit to every direction our hearts desired—from the classic Chanel tweed to a sleek Prada pantsuit.

Donna Karan has keenly observed that clothes are investments. Of course, this is also a great way to justify her prices, but she is definitely on to something! But I would paraphrase her comment just a little.

Clothes themselves are not an investment; it is what you do with the clothes that matters. They will either pay dividends for you or merely make designers rich.

The point: You can use how you dress to help you achieve your next career objective.

Style and Substance

So subtle, so subtle, thus you are formless.
So mysterious, so mysterious, thus you are soundless, thus you hold your enemy's fate in your hand.

Think of style and substance as formless weapons you can use in your career battles. In our attempt to win social and economic battles, the most successful women have found combining substance with style to be unbeatable.

In the workplace, substance is essential, but career success does not depend solely on substance; it also depends on perception. And what you wear can play a large role in how you are perceived.

You may really enjoy dressing like a Raggedy Ann doll with mismatched clothes, or consider it a statement of feminist self-expression, but don't forget that, for the time being, you are still living in a world where business attire has been defined by men.

You will have problems accomplishing your career objectives if your boss or clients consider you unprofessional.

> Style is the packaging for a product; your substance is the product. You need both.
>
> Unless you create an appealing package for yourself, nobody will ever get to know the substance beneath the exterior.

Many working women possess more substance than style. The good news is that it's easier to acquire style than substance. This is why television fashion makeover shows are so popular; with proper tutoring, any woman can be transformed instantly. Gaining substance, however, is far more laborious.

Since every other chapter in this book focuses on substance, here let's focus on why it is important to cultivate an enchanting style—and how to do it. It is easier than you might think. As the saying goes: "There are no ugly women, only lazy ones."

Style Is a Preview of Who You Are

The first step toward enhancing your style is the awareness that it all begins with good health. I can't stress enough the importance of eating right, exercising, and taking good care of yourself.

This is especially important when you are young. When you are young, you can get by skipping sleep, eating junk food, and ignoring exercising. Unfortunately, as you get older, it all catches up to you.

But the converse is also true. If you take care of yourself when you are young, you will always look far younger than you are.

But that's not the only way good health pays off. In our health-obsessed society, there are countless opportunities to build exercise, diet, or fitness-based businesses. Take exercise guru Denise Austin or celebrity trainer Kathy Kaehler. One of the reasons these women have been so successful is that you can tell simply by looking at them that their ideas about fitness and diet work.

You do not have to be born beautiful and a size four to be stylish. Style is not only about the way you dress; it is also about your attitude, your facial expressions, your body language. Your style projects who you are and where you are going.

Style may be mystical and hard to define, but it will always pay the bills for those who are smart enough to cultivate and possess it.

Be Your Own Stylist

I cannot tell you what is the right style for you. That you have to find out for yourself. Once you do, your style can serve as a personal calling card. Anna Sui has so brilliantly linked her boutiques and perfume bottle designs to her personal style that it's impossible to see purple and black without thinking of her vibrant rock-'n'-roll inspired line. Betsey Johnson, too, has made a name for herself by breaking all the rules with her outrageously bright outfits. While some might consider Johnson over the top, others love her sense of fun; whatever your taste, you can't doubt her success.

But remember that Johnson works in an industry where eccentricities are rewarded. If you work in a conservative, male-dominated environment (for the time being; maybe things will change in the future), suppress your urge to dress like Betsey Johnson—unless you own the company.

Finding the style that fits your state of life takes some experimenting, and that can be very costly.

Fashion consultants and image makers are not foolproof. You have to pay for the clothes plus their fee.

Being stylish does not mean following trends blindly. Develop an artistic eye by studying, reading, window shopping, and experimenting. (You can have some fun while doing it.) But find your style, because it will always play an important role in your life.

The "No-Rule Dress Code"

The struggle for survival will give birth to a new force.

During certain points in history, women have worn corsets tightened to the point where we almost passed out. And we had to push our boobs so high that they almost touched our chin. All this to please the male fantasy about how we should look.

But we have paid our dues and earned the right to dress any way that pleases us, whether that means burning our bras or buying matching panties. The only rule about what to wear today is that there are no rules. Given that, here's what you want to think about the next time you get dressed.

> Dress for what you want to be, not what you are.

Everything—including the way you dress—should have a purpose. Since you must wear clothes, make sure they work to your advantage. The clothes you wear not only tell people who you are, they also express what you want to be.

We all want to wear clothes that make us feel natural and comfortable. But if the clothes you feel most comfortable in are not right for your career, you have to think twice.

If you are most comfortable in clothes that flaunt your

breasts and show off your long legs, and your career allows you to do so, by all means figure out a stylish way to do it.

However, if your career objective is to become a Supreme Court justice, wearing plunging necklines and miniskirts is not going to work.

Something has to give.

Designer Ralph Lauren has remarked that, to him, style is about appropriateness.

Whether your clothes are in good taste or bad depends on your objectives. If you want to be a rock singer, don't look like a nun—unless you're going for the I'm-so-unhip-I'm-hip look. If you want to be CEO of a conservative accounting firm, you might considering losing the eyebrow ring or covering your tattoos.

Your Clothes Should Serve You

Your clothes must help you achieve your next objective. Always ask yourself, "Is this style taking me closer to where I want to be?"

I have seen women dress in cheap shoes and clothes, sporting a hairstyle that can only be described as a mess, complain, "How come I can't get promoted?"

You have to look the part before you land the part. Actors know this. They dress in character at auditions, so casting directors don't have to imagine how they will look in the role.

Help others to see you fit in the place where you want to be. The more you look the part, the likelier it is that you will get it.

How to Make Your Clothes and Style Earn for You

1. *A style makeover is the first step for a career makeover.* When Katie Couric left NBC's *Today* show to become an anchor for the *CBS Evening News,* all eyes were on her—and not just on her credibility as a newswoman, but also on her role as a style icon.

In Olivia Barker's August 2006 article in *USA Today,* style gurus weighed in on how she will adapt her day look for the evening news hour. But don't expect Couric to turn into "some bland anchor," says Stacey London, cohost of TLC's *What Not to Wear.* London notes that Couric's fans "will want her to retain a sense of personality and style, because that's what she's beloved for," and adds, "We'll look back and say she was the first to show us how a woman can dress in a way that's really stylish," and still command authority.

2. Before you open your mouth, style speaks for you. Arielle Ford is the publicist responsible for making some very high-profile authors famous. She says that when an author appears on television, it is not what she says that sells books; instead, sales depend totally on whether the audience likes her or not—a reaction that often has a lot to do with physical appearance.

It is common knowledge that during a job interview, the decision to hire or not is made by the interviewer during the first thirty seconds. Whether they admit it or not, many managers are not merely weighing your qualifications when they interview you; they're also wondering "Will this person fit in here?"

Style speaks for you and about you before you even open your mouth.

It Is All About Dressing for What You Want to Be

Enjoy the makeover process.

After reading this chapter, you may think you need to empty your bank account to buy all the latest things. You don't. Learn to mix new pieces with your old classics. Be creative.

Just make sure your clothes produce a return on the money you spend on them. Remember this Chinese proverb: "Humans depend on clothing to stylize themselves, as the statue of Buddha depends on gold to glorify it."

REFLECTION

Think of someone in your office or industry whose style you admire. Look for someone higher up in the organization than you. What is it that works about her style? How can you learn from her judgment about what's appropriate for your line of work while creating a style that is in line with the person you want to become?

CHAPTER 7

Conflict
Don't Show Your Hand

Sun Tzu believed that the key to victory was to get the enemy to reveal as much as possible, while keeping him or her in the dark about your plans, abilities, and knowledge.

Once you've gathered the information about your enemy, use it to buttress your position. You don't have to be the first person to make a move, but by taking this approach, you will be the first to achieve your goal of self-protection.

Most women are surprised to learn that this same strategy—with a little bit of adaptation—can be used to overcome two obstacles that many of us will inevitably face: office jealousy and sexual harassment.

Strategies for Overcoming Office Jealousy

*Ponder and evaluate the specific situation,
then make the moves accordingly.*

The quote above is one of the best-known phrases in *Sun Tzu's Art of War*. The essence of the statement is that there is no one-size-fits-all strategy. Every situation is unique, and we need to find solutions accordingly. As I've mentioned before, studying strategy is not about finding fixed formulas and adopting them to your life. For this reason, Master Sun's words are elusive and leave a lot of space for us to ponder. His strategy is not a "how-to"; rather, it is a philosophical guide for the infinite possibilities that exist within our everyday lives.

Master Sun's strategic thinking is meant to stimulate your mind so that eventually you will be able to toss the strategies you have learned in the air. Doing this leaves you with a philosophical wisdom that will allow you to think on your toes when unexpected events occur in your life.

While our individual lives are different, in this chapter we focus on one common experience of all working women: office jealousy.

If you work in an office filled with politics, jealousy, and backbiting, you may feel as if you've been flailing about in a small tank filled with hungry sharks.

Invariably, the most vicious sharks are female. They seem to have no problem if a man is promoted, but just watch what happens when one of their sisters gets the corner office. I have never understood this. I have attended and spoken at hundreds of women's conferences over the years and really enjoyed them. The meetings are always filled with loving and supportive energy. But all that good feeling that we have toward one another seems to exist only in an artificial, nonthreatening environment, such as the conference. When the weekend's over and we go back to work, the feeding frenzy resumes.

I have witnessed this again and again, from Australia to Europe, in the United States and across the Pacific. This behavior spans cultural and geographic boundaries. No matter where you look, it is always the same. We may (on the surface) appear to be nice to one another, but somehow we feel it is necessary to undermine each other as a part of the unwritten rule of competition in the workplace.

Here's what happened recently in one of my women's workshops, when I asked the thousand-plus women executive attendees, "Who is the enemy?"

The answers in order were:

- Myself

- Other women

- Men

No wonder 80 percent of executive positions are filled by men and only 20 percent by women.

The Crabs-in-the-Pot Syndrome

In an effort to keep each other down, women seem to have fallen prey to something I call the crabs-in-the-pot syndrome.

When you cook crabs, you don't have to place the lid on the boiling pot because the crabs keep one another from getting out. As one crab gets near the top and attempts to climb over the edge, another crab will naturally pull it down in its own attempt to escape. As a result, all the crabs go to their collective doom.

> It is human nature to feel jealous or envious of those who do better at the game of life than we do. Only saints and idiots have been spared this torment. But the fires of jealousy burn away our own mental peace.

But it doesn't have to be that way. There are countless examples from history of women who have risen to the top because they've helped other women excel.

At the turn of the twentieth century, for example, the screenwriter Frances Marion went to New York City, then the film capital of the world, to make her mark. Mary Pickford, the biggest star of the day, immediately recognized her talent and insisted on having Frances direct her next film. The studio resisted. Pickford sent the studio an ultimatum: If you don't let Frances Marion direct my next film, there will be no next film.

With Pickford's support, Frances Marion went on to become a pioneer filmmaker. In a lifetime dedicated to the film business, Marion, in turn, helped many others—including Greta Garbo—become stars. A great number of women have always been, and will continue to be, tremendously helpful to one another.

But that doesn't mean you won't come up against some crabs in your quest for success.

Strategies for Overcoming Office Jealousy

> The success of a military action is deeply rooted in deception.

If you are troubled by some nasty, crablike creatures at work, try the following strategies.

1. *Give the illusion you are outside the pot.* This idea ties back to Sun Tzu's core belief that the success of a military action is rooted in deception—keeping your opponents in the dark.

I do not want to leave you thinking that by "deception," Master Sun meant "to deceive." There are deeper meanings to the concept of deception that are important to address here. Once you understand the true spirit of deception, you can adopt and translate this powerful concept into effective action without being viciously deceitful to others.

According to Sun Tzu, the easiest route to victory lies in using the power of misleading your enemy. It is about manipulation of real and unreal to camouflage your strength and weakness. You can use pretended weakness to play into your opponent's hand. When your opponent cannot recognize your strength versus your weaknesses, then you are in control of your opponent's fate.

To the western mind, good and evil, black and white, are usually clearly divided. You are either good or bad, right or wrong, superior or inferior. In the eastern way of thinking, however, everything is relative and not absolute. Nothing is purely bad or good. A knife can be used for healing, but it can also kill. The evil is not contained within the knife but in the intention of the knife handler.

That is why, although the Taoist symbol is the circle divided into black and white, in the black section there is a tiny circle of white and vice versa. Being naively blissful is not bliss. Falling victim to others is not a good measure of virtue. Deception is an effective tool for self-protection.

Just as crabs can pull on only those crabs that are within the same pot, people can direct jealousy toward you only if you allow them to become close to you. The closer a person is to you, the more likely she will be able to harbor destructive thoughts about you. So, be sure to keep a mental and physical distance from the aggressive crabs around you. Do not expose yourself to their viciousness by becoming "buddy buddy," or overly friendly, with your office coworkers. The friendlier you are, the more you look like a crab in the same pot.

If you are pleasant while maintaining a mental distance, you create both a sense of mystery and an illusion that you are outside the pot.

2. Slap her twice the first time she steps out of line.

> Keep your plan as dark as the night. When you move,
> be as unpredictable as the thunderbolt.

While the Good Book says to turn the other cheek when you are mistreated, it also teaches us about an eye for an eye. That is the part you want to concentrate on when it comes to office jealousies. You need to stop the attacks on you right at the beginning. Instead of turning your cheek, slap the offender twice (figuratively, of course), and you will never have to deal with a situation that could, in time, grow out of all proportion. Surprise your offender by following Sun Tzu's advice: Strike back hard and unexpectedly. When you slap back with your words, make sure your spirit is firm, powerful, and immovable like a mountain, without a smell, without anger. And *never* raise your voice.

3. Support a coworker.

> There are two elements that are difficult to achieve.
> One, utilize indirect methods to achieve a direct objective.
> Two, turn misfortune into advantage.

By supporting a capable coworker, you effectively turn competitive misfortune into a career advantage. Support that brilliant, talented lady who is now working under you. (Yes, the one you feel threatened by.)

Here's why. Even if you don't support her, if she has inherent ability, she is going to thrive anyway. She may well get promoted over you, or you may find yourself working below her at a different firm years from now. Refusing to recognize her talents and help her develop them is going to make you look small-minded, jealous, and easily threatened. It's something your boss will notice now—and the rising star will remember later.

Even if you don't end up working together, that talented individual may feel frustrated due to your attempts to hold her back and may take a job with one of your competitors. If she's as good as you fear, she might end up taking away your business.

Vanessa was the editor-in-chief of a women's magazine where Amy was working as a senior editor. Vanessa did everything she could to try to block Amy from being recognized for her extraordinary talent. When she couldn't take it anymore, Amy reluctantly took a new job as editor-in-chief with a smaller women's magazine that had just been launched.

You can predict the ending. Five years later, Vanessa's publication was struggling and was sold to the parent company of Amy's magazine. Shortly thereafter, Vanessa was fired. She is now working in a much less prestigious job for a fraction of the pay.

Take a chance and support another woman. By doing the right thing, you may just be saving your own skin. A word of caution, however. Make sure you do not demand her instant "appreciation." If you do, all is lost because you have already collected your payment. When you give your unconditional support, the "payment" will come back to you with generous interest.

4. *Learn to pick the sweet fruits from the tree of office jealousies.* As Sun Tzu's statement in chapter 3 tells us, it is vitally important to master the ability to utilize indirect methods to achieve a direct objective.

The first and foremost direct objective in our lives is not to get promoted or make more money, but rather to be the best human being we can be. Yet the only way to achieve this objective is by indirect methods—the lessons and the pains we gather along the way of living.

As Mong Tzu, a great Chinese philosopher once said, "When the universe intends to glorify an individual, she must first go through extraordinary hardship in body, mind, and spirit. Then she will be ready to take on great tasks." This is a principle all Asian intellectuals adopt. Nothing that ever happens to us is bad for us if we know how to catch the sweet fruits of the lessons. Nothing ever happens by accident. If an unpleasant event happens to you, that is the universe's way of telling you where you need to change and refine your character. Through trial and tribulation we strengthen our spirit and expand our ability for tolerance. Eventually, the minor event of office jealousy will be like an ant crawling across your hand. You just brush off the incident with your mind. When the offender cannot offend you no matter how she tries, you have taken the fun out of her vicious game and all the power out of her soul. This is the best strategy to manage office jealousies.

Transform Jealousy into Admiration

On your way up, there will always be women attempting to pull you back down. No matter how vicious they are, as long as you hold to your inner vision and see yourself as the innovative, adaptive, and creative woman you are, no person or circumstance can hold you back.

As a group, we women had better wise up. It is in our interest to help other capable women get out of the steaming pot first, so that they can turn around and help us all escape.

It is easy to feel resentful when you see someone else who is better or more successful than you. Get over it. Use their extraordinary achievements to push yourself to achieve beyond your capability.

REFLECTION

Is there someone in your office you feel jealous of? How can you turn your negative feelings into positive ones?

What is it about him or her that you admire?

What lessons might the person be able to teach you about work style?

_____

_____

_____

_____

_____

_____

_____

_____

_____

7.2

Kick Some Butt with Your Jimmy Choos: Dealing with Sexual Harassment

Do not engage an enemy whose ranks are in perfect order. Do not attack a majestic army. This is the way of mastering the art of circumstances.

Sun Tzu makes a statement similar to the one above in his fourth chapter. *When your forces are in an inferior position, move to defense;*

when your forces are superior, move to offense. The point he is making is that you should never cross a strong opponent.

If you are low on the organizational chart—the quintessential definition of being in an inferior position—and you are treated badly, there is little you can do other than to adopt a defensive position and try to protect yourself. (I will explain exactly what that means in a minute.) If you keep yourself from suffering additional harm, consider it a victory. You will have to wait until you are stronger before you can seek justice.

Despite all the progress we have made, and all the laws that have been passed, sexual harassment is ubiquitous in the workplace. No matter how many laws are created to protect women, there will always be some pitiful men who derive feelings of power from making vulgar sexual gestures or remarks.

"I can't think of a professional woman I know who has not experienced some sort of sexual harassment," said Ellen, the vice president in charge of European, Middle East, and African operations for a Fortune 100 company. "When I was going to college, I worked for a large department store part time. One day my boss asked me, 'When did you discover your clitoris?'

"I went home and cried. I desperately needed the money to pay for school so I couldn't quit. I had to stick it out. I tried to avoid my boss every minute of every day that I remained there.

"I joined another company after graduation. At my first meeting as a member of the almost all-male department, my general manager stood up and said, 'I want to introduce Ellen. I am just delighted to have her join us.'

"He went through my credentials and I thought to myself, how lucky I was that he would take the time to make sure I got off to a good start. I was sitting in the back of the room and he asked me to stand up to be acknowledged. I am modest; so I stood up and sat down quickly.

"He asked me to stand again, and then he said, 'You can see

why I am so pleased that she joined our organization. She is one heck of a good-looking chick.'

"What he was saying in front of the 250 men was:

1. She is a good-looking woman;

2. I am pleased that she is here because she is good-looking; and

3. I give you permission to think of her that way.

"I can probably tell you fifteen stories like that one. In those days we didn't have any kind of help regarding sexual humiliation."

Thankfully, today we do. Women like Ellen have paved the way for younger women by enduring these kinds of humiliating experiences and eventually doing something about the problem.

"As I got a bit older, and slightly higher in the organization, I began speaking to jerks like this. I explained that their behavior creates issues for me, and, if they did this to other women, it would create an issue for them as well.

"Then I'd add, 'You are lucky that I am not a litigious-minded person,' and that there are women who would see this as an opportunity not to educate, but to litigate.

"This would make clear to them that:

1. Don't do this to me;

2. You're putting yourself at a great risk with other women;

3. As a senior person in this organization, your job is to set an example.

"Interestingly enough, when I started to move up to the director and vice president levels, these kinds of things stopped.

When a woman gets to a certain level, men know not to mess with her because she will have the power to come after them.

"People will look at me and say, 'She is powerful; she is successful in a male-dominated engineering company.' But what they don't know is that I have a place in my heart which is full of anger about the years and years of sexual harassment I had to endure. To succeed here, I knew I could not sue, I had to endure. In the end, the endurance has allowed me to achieve what I hoped to achieve."

> Until you point out to men the conduct you find offensive, they will keep doing it. If you tell them, there is no guarantee that things will change. But if you don't, I can guarantee you that they won't.

When You Are Low on the Totem Pole

Ellen climbed her way up the corporate ladder by enduring the pain. Luckily, you don't have to.

1. Keep good records.

> When a warrior is skilled in defense, it is as if she hides in the ninth level of earth, so deep that no man can reach. When a good warrior is skilled in attack, it is as if she moves freely at the ninth level of sky where no man can harm her.

In the statement under 7.2, Sun Tzu told us to not provoke a strong opponent. So, before you take the offense, make sure you cannot lose. Defensive actions come before offensive ones. Keeping a good record of your offender's actions and your experiences with him is like hiding under the ninth level (deep) of earth. This can be an effective tool to secure yourself against his smear of your good reputation when you start to bring him to justice. These records also serve as your offensive weapon.

After a three-day workshop in Australia, a woman approached me, crying profusely. She thanked me for what I had said about how to deal with inappropriate behavior from men and explained that she was fighting one of the largest companies in Australia for sexual harassment. After an exhausting three years—during which she suffered from constant debilitating headaches—she won her case. The only reason she did so was because she had kept very detailed records—complete with dates and times—of the specific details of harassment.

She could also show, thanks to her medical records, that whenever she was harassed, she would experience terrible physical pain. Without these records, she would never have had a chance.

Even if you don't choose to sue anyone, you should always keep very good records of any situation that makes you feel uncomfortable or threatened. You never know when they may come in handy.

2. Get a dynamic résumé ready. When Sun Tzu's father failed in his attempt to overthrow the ruling families in Chi, Sun went to Wu to hide. While there, he spent twenty years writing *The Art of War.* You, too, should prepare your résumé *before* you engage a strong opponent.

After you have explained, in no uncertain terms, the behavior you find offensive, and have documented when it has occurred, it is time to start looking for a new job. Even if the man in question has apologized, it does not mean all is well. He might find an opportunity to retaliate.

3. Mimic the power of nature.

Thus one should move as swiftly as the wind,
as gently as the forest, as destructively as the fire.

This is a description of a powerful army or a highly esteemed individual.

Sexual harassment intrudes upon your physical and mental privacy, even if you take steps to end it. You do have a lot of rights and are protected by law, but sometimes, even if you win the case, you lose. Some employers might be afraid to hire you. Colleagues may applaud you for your courage privately, but knowing you're a "troublemaker" and not afraid to sue, they may tend to stay at a respectful distance.

And, of course, even if you put forth significant effort, you may still lose the case.

When you have a strong sense of who you are and strong self-esteem, even if you lose the case in court, you know you are never less as a person and that sexual harassment can never destroy you.

4. *Sexual harassment will not ruin your life, unless you let it.* Nobody's life gets destroyed because somebody pats you on the shoulder or on the butt. It's painful and humiliating, but don't listen to the media outlets in desperate need for the next victim. The reality is, that kind of behavior results from someone else's ignorance or cruelty. It's up to you to be the "bigger woman" and walk away.

> Sexual harassment cannot diminish or damage your self-esteem unless you let it.

5. *Don't press the issue to the extreme.* Sincere compliments are not sexual harassment. Saying "That is a pretty blouse" is not the same as saying "I'd love to see how you'd look in a wet T-shirt." As long as your male counterpart acted gentlemanly, you should take him at face value. Why read his intention as threatening when it might be completely innocent?

6. Don't go out of your way to wage war.

Military maneuvering has its gains as well as its dangers.

If you increase speed by a hundred in order to gain expected advantages, in the event of an unexpected happening, your three commanders could be captured by the enemy.

One of the rules of marching is that only one-tenth of the strongest soldiers will arrive at the destination in a timely manner.

This could leave your commanders exposed to capture.

As Sun Tzu told us in the opening of his book, "War is a serious business." So is a sexual harassment lawsuit. Master Sun is telling us not to go out of our way to wage war and seek gains. The cost may just turn out to be too great. Even if you win, you could end up a loser.

During the lawsuit, your mind has to be in a state of pain in order to convince yourself and the jury that you are a permanently damaged person and to justify the collection of a monetary award. Thus you will become your own prophet and will turn yourself into a permanently damaged individual. No amount of money is great enough to compensate for losing the joy of living. This is as stupid as a general who considers only what is to be gained without considering possible losses.

Research First

Although this book is not intended to be a primer on how to handle sexual harassment, I can point you to several resources:

LawGuru.com provides answers to many of the most frequently asked questions you might have. Go to:
www.lawguru.com/faq/16.html.

Employment-law.freeadvice.com is another helpful Web site. Go to:

http://employment-law.freeadvice.com/sexual_harassment/.

And while the standard advice many people give is "If you think you have been a victim of sexual discrimination, contact your state bar association for a list of attorneys who specialize in that area," I don't think that suggestion is very helpful. You just don't know if those lawyers are any good.

A far better approach, I feel, is to do a little research. Find a plaintiff who sued successfully in a case similar to yours and find out who her attorney was.

But remember, don't wage a war unless you have to.

CHAPTER 8

九変

Imagination
See Things No One Has Seen

C hapter 8 of *Sun Tzu's Art of War* calls on generals everywhere to be innovative and adaptive, to ignore the thinking that came before, to remain flexible in the face of change.

Today the phrase "use your imagination" has become so commonplace that we forget creativity wasn't always celebrated. When Sun Tzu lived 2,500 years ago, it was a radical concept. For example, the conventional wartime strategy of the time was to destroy and conquer without discretion. Master Sun saw the folly of this kind of warfare and advised a more tactical approach:

There are roads which you should not follow, armies that you should not attack, towns which you should not besiege.

Land which you should not contest, commands which you should not obey.

Master Sun was able to see things no one had seen because he thought in unconventional ways.

You can, too, by using your imagination to its fullest.

Let's see how.

8.1

Transform Your Blue Puppy into a Golden Muse

Fragility has its value.
Brutality has its place.
—TAI GONG WONG (SUN TZU'S MENTOR)

Sun Tzu's eighth chapter has baffled scholars for centuries. The title consists of the two Chinese characters for "nine" and "changes." Yet, in the text, no matter where you look, you will not be able to find nine of anything! Students ultimately determined that Master Sun uses "nine" as a symbol for "infinite" because nine is the largest digit in the Chinese numbering system.

Master Sun believed in using creative and innovative tactics to overcome the infinite number of challenges of a battlefield. So, too, must you use your imagination to pacify the war within your mind and your ever-changing mood.

When did everyone become so obsessed with being "perky," up-beat, and happy all the time? In our happiness-obsessed culture, even a lack of a smile might cause people to think there is something wrong with you. What's worse is when we buy into it ourselves.

Human beings come equipped with tons of different emotions—not all of them joyful. When we force ourselves to be happy all the time, we set ourselves up for self-criticism and a state of eternal unhappiness, because it is impossible to live up to such standards. No one can. I know many professional motivational authors and speakers who, when the spotlights go off, are more miserable than you or me.

Sun Tzu warned against excess, explaining that extreme behavior—even good behavior—would always lead to an army's defeat. If you *try* to please everyone all the time or to stay upbeat at all costs, you will bring about your own unhappiness. Even good intentions can bring bad consequences.

So what do you do when you are feeling sad, unhappy, or lethargic? You use those emotions. Nothing in life is ever wasted; all you have to do is to know how to turn these feelings into fantastic opportunities.

Think of the moments you feel sad or frustrated as a blue puppy that you need to play with, and before you know it, your blue puppy will transform itself into a golden muse of inspiration and creativity.

Turning Blue Moments into Golden Opportunities

1. *Acknowledge them.* You are human. Humans have bad days. Therefore, you will have bad days. Start by accepting them.

2. *Rejuvenate.* There are four seasons for a reason. In winter, Earth rests to prepare for spring's rebirth. Trees lose their leaves, bears hibernate. Fortunately, bears aren't encouraged to take a motivational training course. Otherwise, with their newfound "wisdom," just before the deep sleep kicked in, they'd be saying "Get up, get up, you lazy bum." Torn between obeying their natural rhythms and behaving "as they should," by the time spring

finally came, the poor bears would be exhausted and unable to survive.

Human beings, too, are part of nature and therefore are subject to nature's cycles. Rest isn't a luxury; it's a necessity.

3. *Understand the power of simmering.* No matter how short it is, you'll always experience a transitional state when you move from one activity or emotion to another. There are numerous examples to be found in nature. For example, water simmers before it boils. Without simmering, there is no boiling water.

Simmering is not the same as doing nothing. Simmering allows you to gather the strength you'll need to complete an activity. Every one of us has had the experience of becoming dramatically more productive after a period of simmering. Before a large project, such as writing a book, I need time to myself. I know when I've built up enough inspiration because I feel like I'm ready to boil. It's only then that I can blast through the chapters.

Everyone has a different simmering style. You might cuddle up in bed and read a book; maybe you watch television, play games on the Internet, garden, or cook. Whatever it is, give yourself permission to be "unproductive." We all need to simmer from time to time. It gives us the strength to become boundlessly creative and wildly innovative.

4. *Honor your blue moments.* Part of being creative means you'll experience moments of sadness; it's what you do with these moments that makes all the difference. Honor your blue moments. How? It's easy; just accept them without judgment. (I'm not talking about clinical depression here; if you are battling a severe bout of depression, you should seek the help of a medical professional.)

But if you only occasionally feel low, it is important to honor your blue moments. Embrace what is natural. You can't fight the cycles of life; doing so will only make you miserable.

> Don't worry if you occasionally feel blue. It is
> nature's way of telling you to slow down and reflect.

Discontentment Is the Root of All Creativity

Discontentment is a blue moment that lasts for an extended period of time. Unfortunately, it won't go away until you fix the underlying source of your unhappiness. You'll often discover that you haven't pushed yourself to accomplish all that you are capable of. Your subconscious knows when you should be doing more. Pay attention to what it's telling you.

You can do two things with your discontentment:

1. You can do nothing. (I don't recommend it.)

2. You can use your discontentment to fuel the motor of creativity.

If you choose option 2, your discontentment can serve as a motivating force that will change your life. When viewed this way, discontentment is a very positive thing, indeed.

Here's why. Creativity and innovation are rooted in the spirit's sense of discontentment. When discontented, the spirit will search for ways to improve its condition by finding a better channel for expressing itself. I saw a television interview in which Bette Midler's husband, Martin von Haselberg, said she agonizes over everything more than anyone he knows. Jerry Seinfeld tells people who ask that he has to live in New York because the constant irritation of life there is a catalyst for his comedy.

Of course, no one wants to live in agony all the time, but it's during these low moments that the human spirit redefines itself. Writers, painters, architects, designers, poets, composers, and comedians cannot create art without it.

Accept the Cycles of Highs and Lows

Women's natural rhythms—the fluctuation between highs and lows and back again—are more cyclical than men's. Rather than fighting this, we should explore its positive aspect. After all, even the high jumper needs to bend down in order to be able to spring upward. Cycles exist everywhere you look.

Every businessperson knows about sales cycles; even the best salesperson in the world has dry spells. Inevitably, when she's experiencing one of these stretches, she'll come up against some criticism. Did she lose her touch? Can she do it again? For many of us, the pain of knowing that others are judging us is far greater than a lack of income or accolades.

Let me set the record straight: Everyone has those low periods; they, too, are part of nature's cycle. Blaming yourself will only make you less effective.

During a Fortune 100 company's international retreat rewarding the top thousand salespeople, when I told the attendees they had my permission to have a slow period in the year ahead, there was an audible, collective sigh of relief throughout the room. Even these top salespeople knew the secret pain that results from months of fluctuating performance.

> The sooner you accept that there will be down periods, the better you'll be able to bounce back.

During periods of low productivity, seize the opportunity to take that vacation—even if it's just a couple of days off to relax and forget about your work. Changing your environment will help you change your mental state; getting "unstuck" will help bring fresh enthusiasm to your work when you return.

This low period is a great time to catch up on sleep, reading, gardening, projects around the house, and all the little things you have to do to maintain your life outside work. How we use our slow times has a direct impact on how effective we are during the hectic times.

Accept the "Nine Changes" of Moods

Not every experience in your life will be positive. But you can use negative experiences and emotions to help you reach positive objectives.

If your goal is to succeed at whatever you try to accomplish, you have to learn to use every experience, including your anger, fear, shame, desire, greed, jealousy, worry, anxiety, hatred. Take that which you cannot change and use it for your benefit.

REFLECTION

Make a list of some of the "negative" moods you frequently experience and stretch your imagination to find creative ways to use them.

EXAMPLE

Hatred

Instead of hating your boss for not recognizing your ability, start to hate the bad habits that are holding you back. Refocus your energy into positive motivation that will push you forward and upward.

Fear

As Eleanor Roosevelt said, "You gain strength, courage, and confidence by every experience in which you really stop to look fear in the face." The way to transform fear into courage is not by avoiding it, or by trying to convince yourself you are not afraid, but rather by doing just the opposite, by entering into your fear, getting to know its shape and color. For example, the only way I overcame my fear of deep water was by taking a diving lesson in the Caribbean Sea. Of course, there is more than one way to handle fear. As the great 13th-century Hindu philosopher Shankaracharya said, "When the bravest warrior is in the midst of the battle, her mind is in fear, her body is in fear, yet she clings to the fearlessness of her spirit and marches forward."

Worry

The next time you feel anxious, focus your attention on that place of heaviness and uneasiness in your heart and breathe deeply into it. Notice what happens to that heaviness when you concentrate all your attention on breathing into that area. You may also find it useful to write down what you're feeling.

_____

_____

_____

_____

_____

_____

_____

_____

_____

_____

_____

_____

Women Are from Venus ... Mars, the Moon, and Earth

There are five dangerous faults that will cause you to fail:

- When you are pledged to die, you are easily killed.

- When you cling to life, you can be easily captured.

- When you have a hot temper, you will make regretful moves.

- When you are attached to honor, you can be easily shamed.

- When you are overprudent of your soldiers, you fall victim to worry.

As I have said before, do not look for consistency in *Sun Tzu's Art of War*. In the passage just quoted, Master Sun says, "When you are overprudent of your soldiers, you fall victim to worry." A more literal translation, taking into account the Chinese language's lack of pronouns or articles, would be "Love people, thus worry." So what do you do? *Not* love your people? This certainly contradicts Sun's advice to treat your soldiers as you would your children. (More about that in the next chapter.)

What he means is that a good leader needs to love her people while also remaining detached from love of her people. Here, as in many other places in the book, the Chinese philosopher embraces the power of paradox.

Similarly, this chapter will demonstrate how your positive characteristics can work for—and against—you.

Once again, Sun Tzu draws our attention to the fact that our weaknesses are directly related to our strengths. Strength and passion can easily dissolve into anger when things don't go our way. Kindness and a desire to please can deteriorate into a wishy-washy attitude. Attractiveness can cause us to ignore our other strengths and rely solely on our physical gifts.

Let me explain. In keeping with the spirit of Taoist philosophy, which, as you will recall, draws lessons from the world around us, I will demonstrate how your dominant temperament, if not kept in check, can cause your downfall.

Remember John Gray's bestselling book *Men Are from Mars, Women Are from Venus*? I would argue that women are much more complex and different from one another to make such a blanket statement true. That being said, in my consulting work, I have come to identify several personality types that echo the traits we often associate with certain heavenly bodies—traits that can take over your personality if you are not careful.

Women from Mars Never Get to the Top

Recently I was invited to do a national television show. I arrived at the studio on time and was greeted by a very friendly staff. I asked for directions to the ladies' room so I could check my camera-ready makeup. I spent, at most, three minutes in the restroom.

As I walked out of the ladies' room, I saw that the woman who would interview me was already seated behind the desk. I was impressed at how efficient she was. But as I glanced around, I noticed that the same staff who had greeted me earlier with a smile now looked intimidated and scared. It became clear to me that their boss, the woman who would be interviewing me, held a tight rope around everyone's neck. But I didn't think too much about it. It is common for people to get uptight when their boss is around.

I took my seat, put my purse out of view, and reached inside to get my hand cream. The room got suddenly still.

"Are you all waiting for me?" I asked lightheartedly.

"Yes," my interviewer said.

"May I just put on my hand cream?"

"Can't you do that later?" the interviewer said in a tone you would use with an exasperating three-year-old.

This was so unexpected. I had walked into the studio less than ten minutes ago—seven is probably more like it. No one could have said I took too long. It often takes a half hour or more from the time you walk into the studio until the cameras start rolling to tape an interview that will air later.

I was happy the woman interviewing me was a professional, but couldn't she wait the thirty seconds it would have taken to make sure my hands feel good and look OK on camera?

My putting on hand cream was not going to make her show fall apart. As a matter of fact, by making me uncomfortable, she was hurting the chances of getting a great interview. Who wants to watch an uptight guest? It was clear why her staff looked scared. She treated everyone this way. Still, I was a guest, so I respected her wishes. I put the hand cream away and smiled at her.

"I'm ready."

During our interview, I mentioned that if a woman felt she wasn't promoted because she was a victim of discrimination, she should think twice. Most likely she needed to improve her technical skills, or had not yet convinced people she was a strong enough leader.

"Don't just scream 'discrimination,' " I said. "Look within."

Here was the interviewer's follow-up question: "If a woman devotes herself totally to her work, even giving up the thought of having children, in order to focus completely on career, and she still doesn't get to the very top, are you saying there is something wrong with her?"

Somehow, I knew she was talking about herself, but I didn't call attention to what I considered her weakness. I didn't feel she was ready to hear the truth. Instead, I said that "that woman" should ask someone who truly had her interests at heart to speculate on why she hadn't been promoted.

The answer I should have given her is "The reason you won't get promoted is because you're from Mars."

Women from Mars lead by intimidation and by instilling fear in their employees. Their bullying ways may get them noticed and in some cases allow them to move up the ladder quickly, but until they learn to loosen up, they will never be trusted with running a company. Their bosses will always be wary of their dictatorial will. If given total control of the company, she would make work a living hell for every single employee.

> The woman from Mars is a nitpicker. Her need for perfection makes her intolerant of everything. She'll never be CEO.

If You Think You May Be from Mars . . .

Mars women are always ready for battle, so they need to learn how to relax. Because that is not easy (to say the least) for them to do, let me offer some suggestions.

1. To loosen up, first you must recognize that you are uptight. Most of the women from Mars don't know there is a problem. They think: "All this attention to detail is a great way to advance my career." Yes, when you are first starting out, self-imposed discipline will get you noticed and promoted. However, the higher you climb, the more quickly this quality will work against you. You will alienate everyone around you—and your boss will notice. So, you need to be aware that the very qualities that advanced your career can become a hindrance.

2. Be vigilant. As soon as you notice you are getting uptight, stop! Acknowledge what is going on, and force yourself to be more generous with others and yourself. Again, this is far from easy. But it might help you to know that the reason you are acting this way is probably because you unconsciously believe that those around you might not be as good at their jobs as you are. You worry that if you depend on them, they will sabotage everything you hold dear. Maybe that's true right now—but if so, it's up to you to train them, not do their jobs. First you must understand that the problem lies with the way *you* think; you are the cause of your fury. Keep in mind that changing the way you think won't happen overnight. It is always easier to blame others instead of yourself.

3. *Start by turning your thinking around.* Instead of losing your head over something that goes wrong at work, discover how that "obstacle" could work to your advantage.

4. *Know that a manager's job is to motivate, not to abuse.* Your employees may have faults. They may not be as good at their jobs as you are at yours. However, as a manager, it is up to you to motivate and improve their performance. Concentrate on discovering what they do best and build on it. Constant abuse has never caused anyone to improve, but a little constructive criticism can be a tremendous motivator.

5. *It is not easy until it becomes easy.* These changes require constant vigilance. But if you work at it, eventually you'll discover there is another way to get satisfactory results. Remember, you work on Earth, not Mars. And on planet Earth, vicious women from Mars never get to the top.

Moon Women Get Taken Advantage Of

Many women complain, "Because I am nice, people take advantage of me." But in fact, nice women never finish last; *wimps* do. And wimps love to glorify themselves by saying they are "nice."

In fact, being nice does not mean you have to be wimpy, and being wimpy does not mean you are nice. Let me draw the distinction.

Being nice and pleasant is a natural state. Wimpiness is an

unnatural state caused by your fear to confront and/or a desire to seek approval at all costs. If you're letting people walk all over you, you're not being nice, you're being a wimp.

> With every first meeting there is a "sizing up." If you reveal that you are a wimp, people will invariably walk all over you.

Barbara is a psychologist in Chicago with no more than two or three patients in any week. Her income is meager, reflecting her lack of effort to build a real practice. Her husband pays the rent for her barely used office and paid off her $30,000 in student loans, facts he never lets her forget.

Barbara often tells me in tears that her husband does not respect her. But respect is not free; you have to earn it.

> You must do something worthy of respect in order to have self-respect and be respected by others.

So what should Barbara do? She's got the degree; she needs to put it to good use. She has the office space—but needs to fill it. If she wants to build her client base, she needs to start publishing articles in medical and psychology journals, reaching out to colleagues who may provide her with referrals, attending conferences, sitting on panels, learning more about specific disorders so as to be of more service to her clients. I guarantee that if Barbara takes a more proactive approach to her career, she'll make back the $30,000 her husband spent on her student loans in no time. No matter what your field, it's not enough to get your degree and sit back and wait for clients to come to you.

In truth, all of us have a certain degree of wimpiness (just as we all have characteristics of Mars women), but you can avoid being a Moon woman by learning to stand up for yourself. Those who don't will always be stepped on.

Venus Women

The women from Venus and the Moon are similar, but there is one big difference. Deep down the Moon woman knows she is a wimp—in fact, that's what holds her back. The woman from Venus, on the other hand, views herself as smart and opportunistic. She understands her assets—her face and body—and how to maximize them—naturally or with the help of a plastic surgeon.

She uses her physical appearance as a general would the geography of rivers and mountains in the battlefield. They are her weapons. But as smart as she thinks she is, there is something that all Venus women forget: There is always a younger Venus waiting to replace her.

The original Venus possessed eternal youth. You do not. If your beauty and your sexuality are your only weapons, eventually you will lose. Of course, the point is, they are never your only weapons; if you think they are, you just have not yet looked inside to recognize what other talents you possess. The good news is, it's never too late to discover your inner beauty.

If you still believe that finding a rich husband is enough to make you happy, consider the following story. During a weekend when I was scheduled to speak to a conference of high-powered (male) executives, I chanced to audit a workshop for their wives. The purpose of this workshop, which was led by a psychologist, was to teach these women how to deal with the stress of being the supporting partner.

One after another, they shared their stories; each boiled down to the same issue: The only one who mattered in their family was the husband. His needs always came first.

"My husband is a CEO of a multinational company," a lovely blonde in her late thirties began. "We've been living in Chicago for the past five years. We have a beautiful home, maids, and our kids are happy in school. One day he came home and informed me that we were relocating to Hong Kong immediately. It was up to me to take care of moving. He didn't ask me if I wanted to live in Hong Kong. He didn't care about how the children would feel leaving their friends.

"Now I am living in Hong Kong in a much smaller home that can't fit most of our furniture."

Her sobs were heart-wrenching but totally disproportionate to the problem she described. What really bothered her was that she was nothing but a concubine in her husband's eyes.

Even though it was the arrangement they chose, these women couldn't understand why their husbands' work took precedence over their own needs.

As I witnessed these twenty or so women weeping, a mental picture surfaced. I realized they were no different from those women thousands of years ago who served as concubines in the emperor's court. Their job was to please and support and swallow their agonies in silence.

The next time you start thinking how nice it would be to quit your job and find a wealthy husband to support you, think again. Ask yourself whether the material gains are really worth giving up your dignity.

Earth Women Succeed

The Earth woman is much more complicated than the others. She struggles to balance the qualities of the women from Mars, the Moon, and Venus with the honest, hardworking woman inside. The balancing act is challenging.

She is disciplined but not abusive. She is tolerant and kind but not a pushover. She can be sensual and beautiful but knows when to put on a suit and go out and kick some butt. The Earth woman is an effective businesswoman who also happens to be a compassionate human being.

She may not be loved by all, but that's okay. She is not trying to be. She isn't phony. She is herself.

She understands that a successful life is about balancing paradoxical forces. If you possess too much of Mars' energy, you are always on the warpath. If you strive for acceptance and are not willing to fight for what you believe in, you will always be stepped on. If you think your beauty alone is enough to take you places, you need to think again.

The Earth woman understands all this; she integrates the forces inside her so that the sum adds up to be much more than the parts. She does not deny the Mars, Moon, and Venus women within her. She maintains balance between these opposing forces, between her own strengths and weaknesses.

REFLECTION

Do you share any of the traits of the women from Mars, Venus, and the Moon? What steps might you take to become a more balanced Earth woman?

_____

_____

_____

_____

_____

_____

CHAPTER 9

Managing the Troops
The Principles of Management

The title for this chapter is Xing Jun. In Sun Tzu's time, *xing* was translated as "to manage" or "to use" and *jun* meant "soldiers" or "troops." In modern Chinese, *xing* means "to walk" or "to march"; many books have translated the title of this chapter as "Marching Troops." These translations are incorrect.

In this chapter Master Sun speaks of how a general in a battlefield situation can deal with miscellaneous issues, such as how to cross a river, where to camp, and how to be aware of ambush.

We will not deal with Sun Tzu's management tactics on the battlefield; rather, we will look at how to manage people in today's workplace.

I follow the spirit of Master Sun's ninth chapter, but pull together text from various other chapters that deals with managing people. I'm certain Sun Tzu would applaud my creative approach to tackling his thoughts on management.

9.1

The Essence of Organizational Management

Managing a large group of people is exactly the same as managing a small group; it is all about the division of numbers.

It took me the longest time to understand this simple statement. I just couldn't grasp how managing a Fortune 100 company could be the same as running a start-up. But one day, when I was managing my own small staff, I got it. The only real difference is a matter of magnitude.

Every detail must be considered just as carefully in a small environment as in a larger one. Every aspect of marketing, systems engineering, accounting, and manufacturing is just as important. The functions are the same.

That is something that women like Judy George, Anita Roddick, and Doris Christopher learned as they transformed their start-ups into retail empires: Domain in George's case; The Body Shop's in Roddick's, and The Pampered Chef's in Christopher's.

But it also works the other way, as well. Connie Duckworth, a retired partner at Goldman Sachs, used the skills she learned at the prestigious investment bank to help create Circle Financial Group, a smaller New York–based firm.

The only difference is that in the large company you may have one hundred people doing the accounting instead of one. The tasks are no longer handled by one person, but rather broken down by departments or divisions. Of course, in a smaller firm, each employee must demonstrate the same skill and attention to detail as a 200-person department.

Whether you are the manager of a two-person department or a senior vice president with hundreds of employees reporting to you, you need to understand your group's dynamic.

> A proficient general directs ten thousand soldiers as if she were holding one individual's hand; she can manipulate both with total freedom.

Just how to do this is one of the biggest disagreements between East and West when it comes to managing.

In the West, companies want to know how many people you have managed in the past. In ancient China, leaders wanted to know how well you understood the art of managing. Actual experience did not matter. Unfortunately, today many Asian managers have embraced the western approach, turning their back on a heritage that proved successful in the past.

And what was the intuitive knowledge that Sun Tzu brought to the art of managing an army? To him, the key to managing a million soldiers was understanding how one individual performs in a given situation. When a million people get together, the group does not have one million personalities; rather, it takes on one personality. If you know how to handle one person, then undoubtedly you can manage a million people as a single unit.

My friend Marie is a personal friend of China's former premier Jiang Zemin. Once, during dinner, they were having a lighthearted discussion about how to manage China. The premier asked Marie, "How would you do it?"

Marie replied, "I would treat the billion Chinese as if they were my children. By following this principle, China would be well."

Which brings us to my next point.

Family and Work Skills Are Complementary

With so much debate over women choosing to opt out of the workplace (as if we all have this "choice"), we often forget how complementary the skills of managing work and life at home can be. Women in fields from advertising (consider Shelley Lazarus, chairman, president, and CEO of Ogilvy & Mather) to the sciences (such as Myrtle Potter, a division president at Genentech) frequently talk about how the skills they learned running a household—time management, interpersonal relationships, and balancing competing needs, to name just three—translate to the workplace.

Good mothers and good managers share five important qualities:

1. *Wisdom.* A mother must be wise in order to provide guidance for her children. Similarly, a leader at work needs both vision and technical competency. She must be good at what she does in order to bring out the best in her people and make a profit for her company.

Understanding, direction, vision, guidance, and proficiency are qualities that you will find in both wise mothers and wise leaders.

2. *Trustworthiness.* A mother must earn her children's trust in order to be able to provide them with a nurturing and supportive upbringing. And, of course, a leader must earn the trust of her people, or they will never believe in her vision. If they don't trust her, they will spend their working hours looking for another job, instead of focusing on their current one. If the leader is not trusted by her bosses, investors, or stockholders, she will not be able to fulfill her vision. Her superiors will interfere and attempt to micromanage her. If she delivers an inferior product or poor service, she will be distrusted by her customers and sales will fall.

3. Benevolence.

Equip your army with nutritious food and ample supplies and position them on sunlit high ground, free from disease, instead of dark, wet low ground where disease multiplies.

When you take good care of your army and they are happy, they will win battles for you.

Benevolence is not being a doormat; it is about radiating personal power and showing an ability to embrace differing opinions. It short, it is a quality that comes from inner strength.

The benevolent mother accepts and understands her children's viewpoints. The mother who mercilessly imposes her values and rules upon her children becomes toxic and abusive.

A benevolent leader is not threatened by criticism; instead she feels indebted to a staff that is honest and direct. A benevolent leader instills a sense of equality among her management team and workers; duties may vary, but opportunity and basic human dignity are equal. She makes people feel good about working for her.

Of course, in your quest to become a benevolent leader, remember not to reward your troops too frequently. As Sun Tzu said:

Too frequent rewards to your troops indicate that you are at the end of your resources; too frequent punishment of your troops means you are frustrated with your condition.

As any dog trainer will tell you, when you give your dog too much unearned affection, you will soon end up with one out-of-control pup. The dog will know it is in charge, that it holds the power. This rule also applies to your children and your staff.

My friend Tina and her husband, Ted, learned this lesson the hard way when their multimedia company fell on hard times. As the competition got tougher, many deals that they were counting on simply disappeared.

In the hope of attracting new business, Ted needed his staff to stay on the job so that the office would look full when potential clients came in for appointments. He wanted to give the impression that the business was thriving instead of dissolving.

Almost every day, Ted would give motivational pep talks and treat his people to restaurant meals or take-out. The more he talked and picked up the check, the faster his employees resigned. His employees could sense his desperation and decided to jump ship quick.

While this was going on, Tina would have ferocious arguments and finger-pointing sessions with Leo, who was in charge of the technical department. The fights were out of proportion to the issues at hand. Obviously, it was Tina's frustration with the failing business that caused her to overreact. Ultimately, the cause of the fights didn't matter. Leo took a job with a (growing) competitor.

It wasn't long before the company went out of business. As I looked at this situation, I reflected on how true Sun Tzu's words are. No good can come of praising or punishing people—our employees or children—when they don't deserve it. As Master Sun said, you need to impose discipline appropriately.

4. *Strictness.* A mother can't expect her children to be disciplined if she tolerates bad behavior. At first, strictness may seem in conflict with tolerance and benevolence; it is not. Of course, when you are strict without compassion, your child will rebel. But if you are not strict at all, you'll spoil your child.

Good mothering, like good business leadership, lies in balancing paradoxical forces: benevolence with strictness, wisdom with ignorance, and courage with fear.

If the guidelines you set as a leader are clear and rigorously enforced, then people will perform. Strictness is not something

146

that applies only to your staff but also to your relationship with your bosses, partners, customers, and especially to yourself.

Nicole owned a small custom software house that never set limits on its customers. It allowed them to demand more work and change the focus of a project time after time, even after a contract had been signed. Eventually the firm went bankrupt. You can work without pay for only so long.

If Nicole's firm had held its customers' feet to the fire, insisting that they stick to what they had agreed to or requiring them to pay extra for alterations, it could have avoided failure.

5. Courage. It takes great courage for a mother to trust her kids and raise them in the way she believes to be right. It is no different for a leader.

A good leader is always willing to consider something new. However, it takes courage to act this way. When you make changes, you face risks and uncertainty and potential failures. That takes guts.

Leaders cannot lead without courage. Whether called on to reach personal goals or your company's objectives, bravery is vital to success. Otherwise, strategic planning is like playing war games on paper. It may be entertaining, but it is not productive.

A courageous leader is not without fear; rather, in spite of her fear, she faces her challenges and does what must be done.

While it is true that leaders cannot lead without courage, you shouldn't accept a leadership position unless you are very competent in your field *and* you can give affirmative answers to these questions:

- Do I possess the ability to be decisive?

- Do I have the guts to complete the necessary tasks?

- Am I willing to take calculated risks?

- Do I have the stomach to handle the unpredictable setbacks?

- Do I possess an uncrushable strength?

- If my plan fails, am I resilient enough to bounce back?

- Do I have the ability to bear humiliation?

- Can I endure trying times?

If your answers to all of these questions is yes, you have the right temperament to become a leader. If the answer to any of these questions is no, you have some work to do before you accept the challenge of leadership.

> Mental strength is vital to the success of every working woman, whether you are trying to attain personal goals or your company's objectives. If you cannot handle the pain of setbacks, don't take on a leadership role in the battlefield of either business or life.

The superior leader is one who can deal with a number of challenges simultaneously—from understanding the people she deals with daily to creating a vision—and have them all come together into a seamless whole.

A good leader at work: plans strategies, translates them into tasks, delegates, supervises the execution, and finally checks the results. She then seeks out areas that need improvement and alters her strategies to provide for a more effective execution in the future.

A leader leads by leading. And that is true whether the leading occurs at work or at home. Of course, the attitude and tone of voice you use will be different in speaking to your staff and your kids, and odds are you won't be writing your children many memos (or maybe you will), but the principles of nurturing, empowering, correcting, and disciplining are the same.

By the same token, if you learn to cultivate your staff's talent and help them to complete projects successfully, you will be able to transfer this experience to child rearing.

Obviously, you must also give your employees the proper training, but when you take care of your people as if they are your children, you will gain their respect and loyalty.

Terrain
Move According to
Your Environment

In Chinese, the two words that make up the title of Chapter 10 of *Sun Tzu's Art of War* translate to "geography" and "shape." Clearly, he was talking about the terrain on which armies have to fight their battles.

We don't do much hand-to-hand fighting in the office these days, but there certainly are political battles we need to fight every day. In this chapter, we will look at office politics from the perspectives of both the employee and the manager and talk about what it will take to succeed and what will cause you to fail.

How to Get Promoted—
Without Trying Too Hard

There are six types of terrain: the friendly terrain; the steep road; the complex terrain; the narrow passage; the hilltop; the distant land.

In an ideal world, everyone would get promoted based solely on her performance. And everyone in your company would support one another so that each might shine in his or her respective area of excellence.

But the reality is, office politics is here to stay.

If you are truly brilliant and hardworking, and yet are still being passed over for the promotions you deserve, you may want to consider polishing your in-office political skills.

For most of us, office politics can cause more pain and stress than the duties associated with our jobs. The anxiety keeps you from doing your work well and stays with you long after your commute home. It can even ruin a wonderful weekend with your family.

But a lack of understanding of office politics will not only cause you emotional anxiety, it can also hinder your career. If you don't know the rules of the game, no matter how brilliant you are, you may get stuck in an inferior post for much longer than you deserve.

The upshot: It is possible to master office politics. I am not talking about making skillful office politics your major objective at work. But simply by knowing what to do in certain situations, you will come to feel more in control, less frustrated, and more agile in avoiding the traps that lie along your career path. All this makes it more likely you will get promoted into ever higher spheres.

Sun Tzu talked about maneuvering through different geographical restrictions. If you substitute "internal political situations" for "geographical restrictions," you will find that the same logic still holds.

1. FRIENDLY TERRAIN

The friendly terrain is where I can come and go freely. I can set my camp in an advantageous position which assures I will have easy access to defense and offense. Such a terrain is also easy to transport supplies and troops through, which will benefit the outcome of the battle.

Friendly terrain is an environment that you can move in and out of with ease. In the office, this means friendly alliances, mentors, great teams. If you are lucky enough to work in friendly terrain, you will be able to achieve your career objectives without unnecessary barriers.

Even though the terrain appears friendly, there are still precautions to take. Always analyze people's motives carefully.

If you need help, make sure to ask someone who possesses the qualities of an ally. Does the person:

- Truly enjoy helping people with no thought of reward?

- Have a special bond with you? For no obvious reason, has this person taken an interest in mentoring you? All of my life I have benefited from this kind of generosity. Look out for helping hands; you'll be surprised at how many of them there are who are willing to help you climb higher.

Conversely, you want to be careful of people who:

- Expect every favor to be quid pro quo. Some people will look out for you only if they think you'll someday be in a position to grant them favors in return. Often they do not state this directly; you will have to use your acute intuition to determine whether people are helping you for less than honorable reasons. Of course, much of business is about reciprocity; but if you help people only when you're looking to get something from them in return, you will not get very far.

- Are skilled deceivers. They pretend to be your ally, yet, for some real or imagined reasons, they see you as a threat. These types of people pretend to support you so they can keep a close eye on you. The simple rule of detecting deceit is: Trust your gut. When your gut is telling you to be wary of your supposed ally, while your mind criticizes you for being suspicious, always go with your gut.

2. STEEP ROADS

The steep road is an inclining road: easy to enter on the downhill, difficult to exit on the uphill. If the enemy is not prepared, you can gain victory through surprise attack. If the enemy is prepared to do battle with you, you will be trapped and cannot retreat. It is often a disadvantageous terrain.

Some job positions are like steep roads. When you want to advance, it is all uphill. There is little internal promotion, so those low on the ladder feel frustrated and higher-ups live in fear of being replaced by some young hotshot. In this kind of terrain, do your job well, but don't let your boss believe that you are a threat to his or her position. Soak up all the knowledge and build as many relationships as you can before looking for another job.

If your supervisor is a luminary in your profession, it's possible that he or she needs more administrative assistance from you than you'd like to give. But don't pass up the opportunity to work for the best because you are afraid of grunt work. Everyone has to pay her dues, and working with someone who is well regarded in your industry will open countless doors in the future.

Even after you have moved on, continue a relationship with your mentor. If your peers associate you with one of the stars of your profession, they will respect you.

By apprenticing yourself to the best, you will make yourself invaluable. You will be viewed as an asset that any other company would love to have.

3. COMPLEX TERRAIN

This terrain is disadvantageous for my army to move in and it is also disadvantageous for my enemy's army to move in. In this terrain, even if my enemy baits me to make a move, I must stay put.

Complex terrain is the truly dysfunctional office. In this environment, the leader's narrow-mindedness, or the impossibility of a project, creates an atmosphere of almost-certain defeat. In a terrain full of mental swamps and political division, it is difficult for anyone to simply do her job, let alone shine.

The trick, should you find yourself in this sort of situation, is to keep your head down and look for another job as quickly as you can. All you can hope for is to survive by not rocking the boat too much.

Here's how an acquaintance of mine, Barbara, escaped complex terrain. After realizing that she could no longer continue to work as an assistant vice president at a printing company—her boss was charming one minute and a maniac the next—she began talking discreetly to everyone she knew in the industry about the possibilities of working elsewhere.

It took far longer than she would have liked—almost a year—and more job interviews than she expected—more than twenty—but thanks to a friend of a friend, she was reacquainted with someone she had worked with years earlier. He had started his own, now-thriving company and hired Barbara to be head of operations at a salary that was 25 percent higher than what she had been making.

4. NARROW PASSAGE

The narrow passage; when I can occupy it first, I will guard the opening to the passage and wait for my enemy. If my enemy holds the passage first and is securely guarding the opening, I will retreat. If my enemy carelessly does not guard the opening, then I shall enter to take the passage.

The narrow passage is similar to a steep road with one distinct difference: It is possible to advance, but only if you are able to occupy a position close to one of the key leaders of your organization. The doors that such opportunities can open for you are limitless. Occupying one of those posts will allow those who hold real sway to see you shine.

If you hold one of these positions, make sure you guard your post well so that no one can replace you until you are ready to move on to better things.

If the narrow passage is already occupied, do not charge in recklessly. The person who is already in this strategic post will—by definition—have the power to harm you, and he or she will do so, if you appear to be a threat.

The only way you can advance in this terrain is if the person who holds this position does not understand the importance of his or her post or defend it properly. If that person shows no sign of retreat, begin talking to trusted peers in the industry about possible opportunities.

5. HILLTOP

When I am occupying the hilltop, I must find an easily defendable spot that provides me with a clear view of my en-

emy's activity. If my enemy occupies the hilltop, I must retreat
or entice them away.

Of course, the best way to survive political maneuvers is by being the boss. It is not that there will be no political infighting
once you reach the top level. Of course there will be. No matter
how high up your position, you will have to fight to keep it. But
you have far more control over the situation when you are in
charge; your lofty perch allows you to see the overall political
terrain far more clearly.

The best way to stay on top is to perform extraordinarily. After all, it took an extraordinary effort to get to the top; now it is
time to show why you belong there.

How you get to the top is what the rest of this book is about.
If I had to summarize it in a phrase, I would say it requires
knowledge of self combined with superior performance and excellent interpersonal skills. Mastering office politics, when you
get right down to it, is really about working well with others.

Never be afraid to work hard. By working hard, you will be
ready when and if your boss is promoted or leaves. While there
is no guarantee you will get the job, you will have doubled your
odds by becoming the most capable, suitable person for that
post.

Having said that, let me add that working hard is important,
but people do not always notice and acknowledge capable, hard
workers. There are times when you need to give fate a little helping hand. How you present your ideas is as important as the
ideas themselves. How visible you are in the organization is as
important as what you do there. And who you've worked with
is often as important as what you've done.

Be sure not to threaten the powers that be. Wait. Always be
genuinely supportive of the ones you serve (and hope someday
to replace). Also, do not fail to support those people below, the
ones who serve you.

6. DISTANT LAND

It is hard to fight a war in the distant land.
It is to your detriment to engage in such a battle.

When the Soviet army waged war against Japan on the battle-field of Manchuria, China, the Soviets were defeated by the inferior Japanese forces. Alexander the Great's attempt to conquer India led to his death. No one successfully wages war in the distant land without a tremendous expenditure of effort.

In the office, the "distant lands" are the people who are many levels above you. Do what you can to create a harmonious relationship with them. Never provoke them.

This is a lesson that Amy Wilkerson learned the hard way. The Manhattan-based CFO of the largest division of a publicly held company, Amy did a terrific impression of the company's CEO, a man with a slight stammer known best for his malapropisms.

Rumor had it that the CEO, who worked in L.A., was actually rather fond of Amy's imitations. What he didn't like was Amy telling anyone who would listen that she could do a better job running the company.

After hearing about this behavior (secondhand) for months, the CEO announced with great fanfare that Amy, who loved Manhattan, was being "promoted." She would now run the company's smallest division—in Kansas.

While her title was indeed changed to "division president," Amy found herself in charge of far fewer people and with a lot less to do since the tiny division practically ran itself.

Amy languished in this new job for almost three years. That is how long it took her to find a new job, one that was practically identical to the one she'd had three years earlier in New York.

Since you are the Supreme Allied Commander of your life and your career, it is up to you to study well these six types of terrain. When you are facing obstacles, first you need to identify what kind of terrain you are in and how you can propel yourself forward.

This chapter is not intended to teach you how to start conflicts, just as kung-fu is not about learning how to start street fights. The highest strategy is to engender peace and harmony among your office coworkers because where there is harmony, there is Tao; and where there is Tao, there is prosperity.

But when conflicts of interest become unavoidable, it helps to know how to defend yourself and win against adversity. This is the creative adaptation of Fa.

10.2

Six Ways to Fail as a Manager

There are six ways you can lead your army to doom. None of these six ways has to do with temporal or geographic conditions. All of these six elements will result in leading your army to death purely due to the ignorance of you, the commander.

Even after you sit confidently in the executive seat, remember that it is as important to know how to avoid defeat as it is to obtain victory. No one likes thinking about defeat, yet without understanding the six key ways you can fail, you leave yourself open for an ambush.

Let's deal with each of the potential traps you will face as a leader.

Six Ways to Defeat

1. Ignorance of your resources. When you do not have a clear understanding of your resource limitations and take on a task beyond your capacity, you will fail.

You can hear that and say, as most people do, "I know my limitations. I would never take on a project or put myself in a situation for which I am woefully unprepared." And yet women do this all the time because we are:

a. Eager to show off our ability to perform.

b. Impatient to be promoted.

c. Unaware of our strengths and weaknesses and how they relate to the job.

Before you take on any assignment, make sure you have the necessary resources. If you don't, get them. If you can't, don't take on the assignment.

Sun Tzu explained in painful detail what would happen if you failed to follow this commonsense advice.

> When the enemy's force is ten times greater, but the commander feels her courage is sufficient to compensate for the immense numeric disadvantage, this commander is throwing her troops into the might of the enemy as if she were throwing eggs against a rock.

2. Managerial incompetence. Sun Tzu summed up this situation perfectly when he wrote: "When the soldiers are superior and the officers are weak, commands and orders are disregarded."

Working for an incompetent manager is frustrating, demeaning, and makes your work unbearably painful. You can't focus your energy on doing your job when you have to spend (a lot of) time defending or questioning your boss. Your manager's lack of competency will eventually bring down the department; don't let yourself get dragged down with him or her.

This situation frequently occurs in family-run businesses when an owner decides to appoint one of his children to take over the business. While some scions work hard to learn every aspect of the business before taking over, others barely pay attention. The latter was the situation that Paula faced when her boss of eight years appointed his daughter to take over his small clothing company in Manhattan's fashion district.

The company was known for making comfortable clothing for women in their thirties and forties, but the daughter couldn't stand the fact that she would be running a company "whose sole mission is to make soccer moms look good."

The daughter—in her late twenties—wanted to design clothes for her peers.

As gently as she could, Paula pointed out that it (a) was a crowded marketplace; (b) wasn't an area the company knew anything about; and (c) would require the firm to replace its sales force.

The daughter wouldn't listen. She spent millions of her father's money designing clothes for the new market; only after the first four lines flopped did her father reluctantly pull the plug.

The daughter soon left to try her hand at interior decorating. The only reason the company survived was because Paula had kept a scaled-down version of the "soccer mom" clothing line running while the owner's daughter was trying to expand the company's vision. Paula's knowledge might not have been popular at the beginning of the daughter's reign, but ultimately her persistence paid off.

3. *Staff incompetence.* Sun Tzu wrote:

When the officers are superior and the soldiers are inferior, during battle, the officers will be forced to throw themselves into the most dangerous duty and will certainly be killed. Thus, this will lead to the destruction of all the troops.

When a commander is leading poorly trained soldiers toward a superiorly trained enemy, her soldiers will see the enemy and, following the blowing of the northern wind, will flee.

If the manager is a good one but the workers are still incapable of producing the desired result, the project will fail.

I once gave a speech on the elite cruise ship, the *Royal Viking Queen*. The *Queen* caters to the high end of the market; a two-week cruise costs over $30,000 per couple. While I was there, the crew's performance was consistently superb, despite the fact that they were dealing with a very demanding clientele.

I asked the ship director, "How do you train the crew to be so polite under such difficulties?"

His answer: "We pay well and we hire the best people." In his line of work, a pleasant personality is the key, but in any job, there are qualities that simply cannot be taught. The right attitude, enthusiasm for the work: These are qualities that no manager can teach you. Only when you've got the right people working for you can training be effective. It may sound obvious, but you don't need me to tell you how many organizations get this wrong.

4. *Playing favorites.* As Sun Tzu wrote:

When the commander is unreasonable, it leads to resentment among her troops. During the battle, each soldier will conduct her own war, instead of obeying the commands. This will surely lead to defeat.

In order for each project to thrive and the department to succeed, support and harmony between the manager and her employees is essential. If the manager ceaselessly finds fault with her people, or if she creates favored and unfavored groups, then the department's staff will not be able to focus on their job duties. Instead, they will have to play along with the boss's mental games, which is a sure way to defeat.

5. Inability to discipline. Although your job title provides the imprimatur of authority and power, the title by itself will not allow you to manage your staff effectively. You must earn their respect.

The lack of power to discipline your people is often rooted in a lack of confidence and direction. If you have not mapped out any goals or steps to achieve them, if you are confused about the priorities of your projects and provide foggy direction, the chaos you create will bog down your entire team.

Sun Tzu put it this way:

> When the commander is weak and lacks authority over her troops, when there are no clearly assigned duties, when there is no structure or organization within the camp, chaos and disorder will dominate and defeat will be certain.

6. A poorly trained manager. Carl von Clausewitz, who, in the nineteenth century, wrote the most important western book on the strategy of warfare, *On War,* said, "One need not understand anything about the make of a carriage, or the harness of a Battery horse, but he must know how to calculate exactly the march of a column, under different circumstances, according to the time it requires."

The same is true of the people who command an office. A manager does not have to know how to do all the detailed work of each employee, but she must have the requisite information about her competitors, understand her limitations, and know how to utilize her resources to obtain the maximum advantage. If you don't have those skills, disaster awaits.

CHAPTER 11

Nine Battlegrounds
Be More Competitive
by Doing Less

The title of Sun Tzu's eleventh chapter consists of the Chinese words for "nine" and "earth"—which refer to the nine variations of ground you will encounter once you have entered the enemy's territory. At heart, the chapter is about which strategies to adopt when you are "encroaching" on someone else's territory.

So what does this mean for us?

Business is all about entering new territories. Strategic marketing is a form of "intrusion" into another's territory; so is personal advancement. In section 11.1, I will explain how to use the Nine Battlegrounds Principle to help you break into a new market, introduce an idea that will replace a preexisting one, or lobby for a position that was previously held by someone else.

In this chapter Sun Tzu also advises us to *"Be like a maiden. When the enemy opens the door, be swift as a hare."* In other words, "Appear less threatening than you actually are. When the enemy opens the door, rush in."

Since Master Sun was writing for a male audience, let's turn the advice on its head. If you want to compete effectively in today's business world, not only do you need to embrace your "feminine" qualities, you also need to learn how to bring out your "masculine" qualities. For this reason, in 11.2, we will take a look at some of the qualities that have come to be regarded as "positive" or "negative," "feminine" or "masculine." Such labels have become absolutely embedded in the battlegrounds of the East and West alike. But it's time to think differently. If this book hasn't already made you think twice about what it means to be a woman—or about the fine line between positive and negative qualities—then 11.2 will do just that.

11.1

The Nine Battlegrounds for Personal Advancement and Corporate Marketing

There are nine kinds of battlefields in a military operation.
These are scattered ground, light ground, competitive ground, open ground, intersecting ground, heavy ground, difficult ground, surrounded ground, and death ground.

According to many Chinese and Japanese historians, Chapter 11 is the most chaotic, disorganized, and unconnected chapter of *The Art of War*. I agree.

Of course, I don't think that the book can be read in a fixed or "linear" way; rather, concepts that are introduced early in the text are soon abandoned and revisited only later—much in the same way that a diary jumps from thought to thought, returning to unfinished ideas only when the mind is ready. Therefore, in order to help you understand this chapter, I have reorganized it thematically instead of adhering to its original stream-of-consciousness structure.

Let's begin.

1. SCATTERED GROUND

In scattered ground there are civil wars. The kings and the lords are fighting among themselves. In this situation, you should not seek battle.

Sun Tzu did not explain clearly why you should not fight in civil wars right away. Only later do we learn:

Although the people of Wu and Yue hated each other for centuries, when they were crossing the river in the same boat and met with storm, they immediately united together as if they were a pair of left and right arms presenting a strong defensive front. At this time, you need to unite your force and with a single mind [be] determined to march into the territory.

Strategy: Let's say your company is thinking of launching your brand in a new country or market; chances are, there are probably already a few brands fighting for precious market share. Do not make your intention and your presence known to them right away. Do your preparation work quietly as they duke it out, then jump in when they're too busy to notice. As soon as they realize they have a common enemy, they will unite to fight you and keep you out. Your plan will crumble before it is even fully launched.

Personal Advancement: If you are interviewing for a job and hope to move up quickly, keep quiet about that until you are hired. If you seem too ambitious before you even begin your journey, you will run into unimaginable roadblocks.

Many bosses want you to know your place and do your job well so their lives will be easier. (Note: You should still be eager and enthusiastic about the job you're interviewing for, but balance that excitement with a humbleness that shows you are willing to pay your dues and perform the administrative tasks associated with the job.) If you seem too eager to move to the next level, you may not get hired. Many companies are looking for a worker bee, not a queen bee. That comes later.

2. LIGHT GROUND

Do not stop marching when you are on the light ground.

Again, the explanation was hidden in the later text. Master Sun explained:

> The light ground means that you have just entered your opponent's territory lightly; you have not established yourself, so the host country competitors can easily kick you out.

Strategy: Whenever you enter a new market, you need to focus your resources quickly toward establishing your brand. If you delay or hesitate before you are deeply rooted in the new marketplace, you can be eliminated easily because customers have not attached themselves to your brand or declared loyalty to your product. When customers are uncommitted, you can fall out of a market as fast as you fell in. Do not halt. Move swiftly forward. The same, of course, goes for launching a new idea or initiative within your company. Don't talk about your plans before you are confident that you can put them into action; move forward in one swift action so that everyone's still paying attention when you report your first success.

Personal Advancement: When you have just been hired, you must do your job quickly and diligently. At first, your boss will not value you; do not give up. Only through diligent work will you become indispensable.

3. COMPETITIVE GROUND

The competitive ground is beneficial for me as well as to my competitors. On such a ground, attack not.

Strategy: The logic of why one should not attack such ground is buried in another seemingly irrelevant part of Master Sun's text. If you are the newcomer, don't go after the most desirable and most profitable territory. If you do, you will encounter strong opposition. You should enter the market through a segment everyone else has disregarded. Brilliant advice.

Wal-Mart is such an example. While many retailers were fighting for the most desirable metropolitan real estate to establish department stores, Wal-Mart went to the undesirable suburbs and made its claim. The company soon became the most successful department store in the United States.

Personal Advancement: Don't aim for the hot positions everyone wants. The hotter the position, the hotter the seat; the higher the expectations, the more people will look to find fault in your performance. In a hot position, you will make all your mistakes under a spotlight. Many people are waiting to see you fall and fall fast. Once you fall from grace, getting back to the top can take years.

Instead, after you have excelled in your first role, ask your boss for new responsibility. Say you would like to try to shape up a neglected department and make it work better. Ask to be the head of a small department no one wants. Do your learning and make your mistakes in private, and turn that department into a shining star. You will enjoy the reflected glory from the department's achievement; on top of that, everyone in the company will notice your hard work.

In this way, the less competitive you are, the more you can achieve.

4. OPEN GROUND

On the open ground, you can come and I can go. We all have the liberty of access. In this ground do not try to block your enemy's way.

Strategy: In this passage, Sun Tzu warns against attempting to block your enemy's entrance into an open ground. In business, think of the free market as a prime example of open ground. It is of no use to attempt to block your competitors from entering a market; they will always find a way in—often, with the help of government antitrust laws. In 2004, the European Union fined Microsoft a record 497 million euros for abusing the "near-monopoly" of its Windows operating system. Microsoft was given 120 days to share programming codes with its rivals to ensure that rival products could be used on computers running Windows.

Personal Advancement: Don't hog all the credit (even if you think you deserve it!). Let your team members shine whenever possible. No one likes an attention-hungry superstar.

5. INTERSECTING GROUND

The ground that is next to three neighboring countries is called intersecting ground. Whosoever occupies this ground should build relationships and create alliances with their neighbor countries. Thus, if you do not know your neighbors' [opponents'] mind-set, you cannot speak of diplomatic alliances.

Strategy: If you are surrounded by multiple competitors, instead of fighting each one, why not try to create a joint venture, syndication, or buyout? If your company wants to enter a new market, why not find an existing business or reputable brand you can join, or buy them out and take over their market? Why fight if you don't have to? However, in order to create partnerships, you need to understand your potential partner's mind-set.

You need look no farther than one of America's most popular corporate rivalries to see proof of a powerful partnership that might have happened—but didn't. In the early 1930s, Pepsi Cola owner Charles Guth approached Coca-Cola with an offer to sell, but Coca-Cola refused. The result . . . well . . . you know.

Personal Advancement: Being professionally friendly at work will take you places, will earn you friends and respect; you'll influence people more effectively with less effort. Even if you are on the top, you still need people to support your cause. Getting to know how your peers think and work and supporting them whenever possible will help create lasting relationships. You and a colleague might decide to create your own company together; your assistant today might be the head of a rival company tomorrow.

6. HEAVY GROUND

Sun Tzu defined heavy ground as the moment

> when the army has penetrated into the heart of targeted territories, leaving numerous cities to its rear. In this case, it is necessary to plunder in order to sustain your army's expenses.

Master Sun also teaches us how to arrive at this heavy ground:

> Enter deep into the territory. Only then should you indicate you are focused and committed to becoming the champion.

He concluded:

> In order to effectively control the opponent,
> you need to capture what they value the most.

Strategy: There's nothing your competitor values more than market share. The heavy ground of a product launch occurs once you have established your brand and earned the trust of the consumers. You have secured your market territory; now it is time to expand your commitment and pour in your resources to plunder the profits of everyone else in the market. After all, taking a handsome profit from your competitors is the reason you started this journey.

Personal Advancement: You paid your dues. You played it safe, played it nice, played a role no one else wanted and still managed to shine. Now you have entered rich fertile grounds. There is plenty of wealth to be collected. Enjoy it. However, beware—when you plunder, your actions may have ill consequences. I know of many politicians who, once they entered the office of their dreams, plundered illegally. Some went to jail; in China, some were executed.

7. DIFFICULT GROUND

This ground includes mountain forests, rugged slopes, marshes and fens. The difficult ground includes all paths that are hard to travel. In this ground you have to move fast. It is a leader's job to know how to negotiate these difficult grounds. She must know how to employ superior guides to take advantage of this difficult ground.

Strategy: When you are finding it difficult to penetrate a market, remember that your competitors are facing the same challenges. In this case, whoever is the first to get through the difficult ground is the winner. It is the leader with superior understanding of the Di (terrain) or the one who has employed the best local guide (or, in our world, the best consultant) who will win.

Today's global village is full of difficult ground. These include cultural taboos and distrust, conflicting business styles, and political and bureaucratic barriers. A leader does not need to know every secret of doing business in every country, but she must have the intelligence to employ the best consultants to guide her through unfamiliar terrain.

Personal Advancement: The difficult ground in your office could be a difficult coworker, client, or boss. I'd argue that difficult people are trickier to navigate than a mountain or steep ground. When you work with difficult people, it helps to seek out someone who is respected by or on good terms with them. Maybe you can have this middleman or woman arrange a dinner or casual event to lessen the tension. (Of course, you should pay for the meal.) Whatever you decide, you should go out of your way to show friendship and support when it is least expected. This could be during an office meeting when others do not agree with the difficult person's proposal. You may want to point out the value of her proposal (although you shouldn't lie about the validity of the project if there is none). Often the people who rub us the wrong way do so because they possess the same qualities as we do, so look beyond the things that bother you and recognize the other person's talent. Learn to be generous with your support; people will remember it and return the favor.

8. SURROUNDED GROUND

In such ground, the way in is narrow and the way out is marked by tortuous paths so only a small number of the enemy would be sufficient to overtake a large body of men. When we are stuck with such a ground, we have to resort to strategy. If none is available, then close any escape passes. Let there be no way out.

Strategy: In the late 1970s, China opened its market to the West. In the '80s and '90s, western companies eagerly entered the Chinese market only to find that they had entered a surrounded ground—competition was fierce and the number of potential customers was still relatively small. There was only one way in (with cash) and one way out (without cash). Companies like KFC and McDonalds that understood that leaving would mean losing dominance over a market that had yet to hit its peak have enjoyed tremendous growth in the Chinese market.

Personal Advancement: What if you find yourself in a position where there seems to be no way out—your new initiative has failed, or your company is in hot water? You can either reach deep into the strategies that you have learned to plan an escape, or you can stay and fight to the death—strategically. Whatever you decide, make sure your decision is in alignment with Tao. This is exactly what Enron whistleblower Sherron Watkins did when she wrote her now-famous memo to former CEO Kenneth Lay, warning "I am incredibly nervous that we will implode in a wave of accounting scandals." Was it the right decision? Consider this: Watkins was named one of *Time* magazine's People of the Year, while the rest of the company went down in flames.

9. DEATH GROUND

This ground will lead you to death if you don't fight. If you fight with all of your might, you will survive. Out of desperation, fight. When soldiers decide to fight to their death, they become a powerful force and will obey your commands totally.

Strategy: Recall the concept of surrounded ground, which I introduced earlier. When you cannot break free of the surrounded ground, it soon is transformed into "death ground." With no escape, you are forced to fight to the death, as so many Fortune 500 companies have done in China—many of them successfully, I might add. When Western companies experienced devastating losses in the 1980s and early 1990s, they had no choice but to stay and fight to the death. The common belief was that since there are over 1 billion consumers in China, eventually the country would have to transform itself from a planning economy to a market economy. The companies that stayed to fight are now collecting deep profits.

Personal Advancement: I don't believe that you work hard and overcome unbelievable difficulties only for a paycheck. Most of us are true warriors, seeking excellence in our careers to prove to ourselves that we are as good as we think we are. Your superiors may not always acknowledge your ability and reward you with the pay and positions you deserve. Nevertheless, you need to fight to the "death" to prove to yourself that you are unbeatable. Even when your body hurts, your spirit is depleted, your mind is tired, there is a force within you that refuses to die and refuses to surrender to defeat. When you and I survive and walk out of the death ground, there may or may not be applause or promotions waiting for us, but in our heart of hearts, we have gained something—the knowledge that we are indestructible. In time, the universe will come around to sing your praises.

11.2

Adopt the Best of Masculine and Feminine Energies

Proper adoption of [masculine] strength and [feminine] softness is about understanding how to use your Di [resources].

Recently I was asked to talk at a large business conference. The other speakers included former president Gerald Ford, then prime minister John Major of England, former congressman Jack Kemp, former senator Bill Bradley, television political commentator George Will, and former star football quarterback Terry Bradshaw.

I was the only woman who spoke. During my forty-five-minute talk, I mentioned that a perfect human being would be half male and half female. In other words, in order to be effective in the world, a woman needs some masculine qualities, and by the same token, a man who adopts feminine qualities will be a better boss, a better businessman, and a better father and husband.

My statement took only five seconds to deliver yet everyone at the conference remembered it long after my speech. Women reacted with emotional exhilaration. While some men loved it, others were offended by the idea that men needed to adopt feminine characteristics to make them better at their jobs and at home. No matter how they felt about what I said, however, it got them thinking.

Why You Need Both Male and Female Qualities

Over two hundred years ago the French government gave the United States the Statue of Liberty as a symbol of the immense vitality, strength, and beauty of our new nation. No one can deny the statue's beauty. Yet while she exemplifies what we think of as a "feminine beauty," her face also clearly exhibits her inner masculine strength and determination.

The world considers Michelangelo's statue of David to be an inspired representation of the highest perfection of man. What makes the statue so wonderful is not just the muscled body, but also its unmistakable sensitivity. What separates a great work of art from a true masterpiece is how well we can recognize our own humanity within it. Whether you focus on its masculine attributes or its feminine ones, there's no denying its powerful beauty.

One day, on a whim, while I was giving an all-woman seminar, I decided to have the attendees shout out the various attributes that they thought were dominant in each of the sexes. With their help, I compiled a list of men's and women's positive and negative qualities. While this list is not in any way scientific or even correct, it does shed light on gut-level prejudices that, like it or not, many otherwise intelligent and open-minded people still possess.

Here's what the women called out:

MEN'S NEGATIVE QUALITIES	WOMEN'S NEGATIVE QUALITIES
Arrogant	Bossy
Demanding	Emotional
Egotistical	Envious
Immature	Gossipy
Insensitive	Indecisive
Lazy	Insecure
Chauvinistic	Moody
Patronizing	Perfectionist
Self-centered	Petty
Ungrateful	Timid

MEN'S POSITIVE QUALITIES	WOMEN'S POSITIVE QUALITIES
Adventurous	Adaptable
Analytical	Committed
Bold	Creative

MEN'S POSITIVE QUALITIES	WOMEN'S POSITIVE QUALITIES
Focused	Empathetic
Generous	Independent
In control	Intuitive
Logical	Passionate
Open-minded	Practical
Straightforward	Resilient
Strong	Sensitive

Rethinking Masculine and Feminine

After looking at the positive and negative qualities ascribed to both genders, I see many contradictions and false assumptions. The list is not about men and women; rather it is about what are traditionally regarded as feminine and masculine qualities.

Certain women possess a great many masculine qualities, and some men are dominated by feminine qualities. We think of emotions such as love, insecurity, fear, jealousy, envy, and shame as feminine, but in fact they are shared equally by both men and women. Females have no exclusive rights to being "overly" emotional.

During one of my seminars, a manager named Pat asked about gaining time management skills; there was just too much work to do at the office. As I kept asking Pat questions, I discovered the problem had nothing to do with time management. The reason there was so much work to do and so little time to do it was because Pat never said no to people who handed over work.

At the afternoon session, Pat had another question, this one about a difficult employee who acted as if she were the department head instead of Pat. I asked Pat some additional questions, and I realized both the time problem and the difficulties with the employee stemmed from the fact that Pat was unable to stand up to anyone else or show any kind of authority or assertiveness.

While reading the story, you probably assumed Pat was a woman. You are wrong. The full name of the person asking me for help was Patrick. A lack of assertiveness is not the sole provenance of women; men possess this quality in equal measure.

Go back through the men's and women's positive and negative qualities and check which ones apply to you. If you find you are short on your masculine qualities, pay attention to a male coworker whose work and style you respect. Select his admirable qualities—maybe he's great at chasing new leads, perhaps he's not afraid to pitch bold, new ideas—and think about subtly integrating them into your personality.

But remember Sun Tzu's teachings: Whether you should be more masculine or feminine depends on the situation you face. You don't want to be locked into one style or another. You need to be flexible.

Believe it or not, your wardrobe can be a big help here. If you feel like you've been coming off as harsh or aggressive lately, you might incorporate a pale scarf or some sexy lingerie underneath your power suit to give you that sense of inner femininity that you need. If you've been feeling too passive lately, try a dark banker's suit. Whatever costume you decide to don, make sure you're comfortable and that it's appropriate. But remember, no clothes can compensate for a lack of inner balance—while looking to change your outward appearance, also look within.

The Best of Both Worlds

In the workplace, merely being capable is not enough. Capable women are a dime a dozen. The one who means business and shows her leadership through a balance of her masculine and feminine power is that rare diamond among a mountain full of quartz.

CHAPTER 12

Attack by Fire
Fireproofing Yourself

When a kingdom has been destroyed, it cannot come back into existence, just as a dead man can never rise. Thus a wise ruler heeds my warning, and the superior generals are cautious, because this is the way to keep a nation at peace and an army intact.

Sun Tzu's twelfth chapter speaks mainly about how to use fire to wipe out the enemy. Since Master Sun lived in the midst of 550 years of civil war, he knew that setting fire to your enemy's camp was one way to achieve absolute victory.

However, at the end of the chapter he warns that fire can destroy kingdoms and kill people. When a kingdom has been destroyed it cannot rise again, and once a man is dead he cannot come back to life again. Sun Tzu was not advocating mindless annihilation of nations and lives, and his brief warning is an exceptionally pacifist statement to include in a book about war.

The message of this chapter is that if you must fight, get total victory. This raises the question: When should I fight, and why do I need to fight?

In section 12.1 we speak of what will happen when people set fire to you and what you can do about it. In 12.2 we discuss how we can adopt the waterlike power of endurance as a defensive and offensive strategy.

12.1

Rising from the Ashes

Move not, unless you can see the Li [benefit]. Use not your troops, unless you can see the victory. Fight not, unless there is danger to your position.

No matter how peaceful and easygoing you are, somewhere out there someone is calculating how to improve their position at your expense. Even a genius like Albert Einstein wasn't spared. Throughout his career, rivals tried to disprove his Unified Theory.

Every one of us will experience unjust personal and professional attacks, be they minor or major.

There is no way to prevent such attacks. No matter how careful you are, a fire can still find its way to your door. Thankfully, these days, in the corporate setting, physical violence is rare. Unfortunately, however, attacks on your reputation are not, as the following story makes clear.

While in her twenties, Vivian worked for a major bank as a supervising teller. She longed to be accepted into the bank's management program, which would prepare her to become a senior manager. But every time she applied to the program, she was rejected.

One day she was summoned by her supervisor, Linda, who said Vivian had been finally accepted into the program, thanks to Linda's recommendation.

The next day Linda didn't come to work. Vivian heard she had suddenly left the company. Vivian was stunned, of course, but not surprisingly, she was more interested in learning when the training program would start. Vivian went to George, Linda's boss, to find out.

"Congratulations," George said. "I didn't know you got in and I don't have any of the details. Let me get hold of Linda."

Later that day George asked Vivian to come to his office. "Linda said there was no such conversation—that you totally made this up."

Nothing Vivian could say would convince George otherwise, since he couldn't see what Linda would have to gain by lying. Vivian resigned from her job soon thereafter. Missing an opportunity for advancement was a small matter compared to the fact that she'd been labeled a liar and an opportunist. It was a black mark that could never be erased. Linda had made sure Vivian had no future in the bank.

To this day, Vivian isn't sure why Linda acted as she did. Was it because Linda's old boss, Bob, had promoted Vivian so quickly? Had Bob's act of pulling rank—and promoting one of Linda's employees—triggered resentment within Linda? That didn't seem to be a strong enough motive to lie.

"Could it be because I'm black?" Vivian wondered. She could not imagine that Linda would stoop so low.

Other people thought it was jealousy. Linda is a short, overweight woman in her early thirties; Vivian is younger, slim, and extremely attractive.

Vivian weighed everything and still could not find a good reason as to why Linda would set her up.

As frustrating as the situation is, it does reflect an awful truth: You do not always know why people do what they do; they just do it.

We may never know Linda's motive, but what we know for a fact is that she viciously set fire to Vivian's good reputation.

Now the question is: What can Vivian do to rise from the ashes of her tarnished reputation? In other words, what can she do to keep the damage Linda caused to a minimum? When Vivian asked me for advice, I gave her three options. Obviously, which strategy *you* choose to adopt will depend on your personality and circumstances.

1. *Set a fire and let it burn.* After Vivian left the company, she was very upset. She wanted revenge. But the fact was, Linda was gone, off to another position, maybe even another city, where Vivian could not touch her. I told her she could write an anonymous article about the incident (disguising some of the details, and the names involved, so as to avoid a possible lawsuit) and post it on the bank's weblog, both to get it off her chest and to warn others interested in the management program to be more proactive about getting nominated. Vivian could share with others what she learned the hard way: that you should never leave your advancement in the hands of one person—make yourself so visible that any number of people in your firm would be glad to help you move forward in your career.

I also recommended that she wait a month or so before posting it, just to make sure she still wanted revenge once she had cooled off.

Vivian did write the article—she decided to take my advice and change the names and details—and the very act of writing helped her heal. She is no longer enduring the pain she went through. And she's learned not to leave her fate in the hands of one—possible spiteful—manager. Today, four years later, Vivian is a human resources manager for a major pharmaceutical company.

2. *Harness your killer instinct.* Vivian could have gone further than simply writing an anonymous post on the bank's Web site—she could have tracked Linda down and set out to destroy her career. But I asked her to harness her killer instinct and channel that energy into something more productive.

To succeed in business, you need to have the will to finish the job. Among bullfighters, there are many who can work close to the horns, displaying great bravery and brilliant technique, but the great bullfighters are recognized by how they handle themselves at the moment of truth: when the time comes to kill the bull quickly and cleanly. The courage to finish the job, that's the killer instinct. It is the power that propels us to take proper actions, keeping us on the path to our righteous objectives.

There is a killer instinct within each one of us. Thanks to societal rules and laws, we find the idea of actually killing repugnant. But nonetheless, the killer instinct is there. We merely have to harness it in a nonviolent way and align it with our goals.

Vivian wanted to know how she could be in touch with her killer instinct without harming anyone or anything.

Strange as it sounds, I told her, "Go home, mix some pancake batter, and learn to flip a pancake in a frying pan."

As you might know, this is not easy.

You start by rocking the pan to create a momentum that will allow the pancake to slide up and down the sides. Once you have built up the momentum, you flip the pancake into the air with enough force to turn it over, and then you catch it in the pan.

If you are timid and concerned that your pancake will fly too high and miss the pan, invariably you won't throw it high enough to turn it over. When it lands, all you'll have is a mess.

On the other hand, when you use too much force, your pancake will probably land on the stove, outside of the pan—or stick to the ceiling (at least temporarily).

When you flip a pancake, you need to pause first and get in

touch with the state of mind that gives you perfect strength, perfect control, and perfect courage. You need to balance your timidity—"What if I make a mess?"—with overaggressiveness—"You just watch the way I flip the flapjack."

Carefully observe your inner state during the moment just before you throw the pancake high in the air to make that perfect landing. When you find that state of mind, think about how to re-create it without the pan in hand. Doing so will help you find the balance you need to cultivate a killer instinct.

Learning to flip a pancake might not seem a particularly profound lesson. Yet there is a truth to the process that transcends the action. It doesn't matter if you're tapping into your killer instinct to bring down a competitor or flip a pancake. In each case, it is about tapping into the state of perfect strength, perfect control, and perfect detachment. These are the attributes you need to fireproof yourself.

3. Identify the Li (gain) first.

> If there is Li to have, then make a move.
> If not, make no movement.

Sun Tzu discusses the importance of "li" or "gain" elsewhere in the book—in his eyes, the potential gain should be the motive behind all military force. In other words, you should never make a move until you can identify the benefit of the intended action.

I told Vivian, "Bring your killer instinct down to a simmer. Let Linda go, but capture the anger you feel about what she's done to you and use it to fight the battles to come."

Not every battle is worth a fight. If you do not fight back against someone who has harmed you, it does not mean you do not have the killer instinct, it merely means you are choosing your battles wisely.

There was no real reason for Vivian to attack Linda with all her might. After all, no real harm had come to her. Yes, she lost her bank teller position, but those kinds of jobs are easy to find. Yes, Linda caused Vivian substantial pain, but Vivian is far stronger as a result.

Choose Your Battles Wisely

As the Chinese proverb goes, "Real gold does not fear the test of fire."

No one has to go for the kill in order to prove she is noble. And if you set the careers of others on fire for your own gain, just wait . . . someone, some other time, will send the fire hurling back at you—only this time, it will be stronger. The cliché is right: When you play with fire, you get burned.

If someone has set out to destroy your good name or your career, trust me: She cannot harm you if you do not decide to be harmed.

Once you understand that, you can choose whether the battle is worth fighting.

12.2

Endurance:
Fireproof Yourself with Water

Those who attack by fire effectively are the intelligent ones.
Those who attack by using water as an aid are the mighty ones.

As Sun Tzu's statement makes clear, knowing how to attack by fire is only half the battle. A mighty general also understands the power of water—after all, in a fight between fire and water, it is water that endures. You, too, can learn how to harness the power of water to fireproof yourself: The secret is endurance. And it is no secret that enduring is an area where women excel.

When she was only fifteen years old, American swimmer Lynne Cox broke the men and women's world records for swimming the English Channel—a thirty-three-mile stretch that she completed in nine hours and thirty-six minutes. In her book *Swimming to Antarctica* (Knopf), Cox describes her extraordinary journey during which she demolished misconceptions about the strength of women. Many people believe that men are superior in every sport, but as Cox proved, women's bodies are actually much better equipped to endure the cold temperatures of open-water swimming.

Not only did Cox help to break down stereotypes by being the first person to swim such treacherous waters as the Strait of Magellan and the Cape of Good Hope, she also was the first to swim the Bering Strait, the boundary between Alaska and Siberia, opening the U.S.-Soviet border for the first time in forty-eight years. As she put it, "The reason I swam across the Bering Strait was to reach into the future, to cross the international dateline, and to symbolically bridge the distance between the United States and the Soviet Union. It was to generate goodwill and peace between our two countries, our two peoples." It was this swim that prompted her to make her swimming about more than simply breaking records but also "to establish bridges between borders."

While not every woman possesses Cox's athletic ability, her story shows that we are capable of accomplishing great things if we put our minds to it. Cox hasn't just proved wrong the people who doubted her, such as one cabdriver who said, "You don't look like a Channel swimmer to me. You're too fat to be one." (Ironically, it is her body fat that helps her endure such grueling swims.) She's also made her amazing abilities a symbol of teamwork (such swims are not possible without the help of trainers and a crew to monitor the swimmer's body temperature), persistence, and endurance.

Just as Cox was able to endure years of grueling training, shark attacks, freezing water, and enormous swells, so every woman is capable of enduring attacks by fire. The secret? By embracing the power of water.

Water's power is rooted in its ability to conquer all on its path—often not by destroying things in an instant but by patiently eroding the land over time. By enduring the hardships that every woman faces, we are steadily breaking down gender inequality, personal prejudice, and political attacks while we silently and steadfastly swim forward.

Taming the Fires with the Power of Water

Unless there is great danger to the nation, one should not engage warfare.

The ruler should never raise the saber due to his hot temper and a general should not engage the enemy due to his anger.

Recently a friend of mine asked, "How can I protect myself against attacks by fire?" My answer was "You can't. The only person who can make sure that no one dares to set fire on you is the one that has absolute power. And no one in the entire world has absolute power." It is a common belief of many that even the mighty Alexander the Great, a man whose army was able to conquer half the world, was ultimately poisoned by his trusted generals.

Whether you're an emperor or an executive, you risk uprisings, revolutions, and coups. If you are in power, you are, by definition, at risk of being attacked by those who desire your power—that is why many of the greatest emperors aimed not to prevent people from attacking but rather to endure despite these attacks. Similarly, the greatest emperors of China stayed in power not by setting other people on fire but by enduring.

Given this, I told my friend, "You cannot prevent these fires, but you can endure them."

There are countless stories of members of royal courts who have tried to usurp the power of their leaders. For many of these advisors and noblemen and women, their high ranks weren't enough. Driven by ego, they wanted absolute power, which, as I said earlier, is not even an attainable goal. So why didn't the kings and queens merely fire these ambitious traitors or put them to death? Sometimes, of course, they did. But in many other cases, they kept them alive out of necessity. Often these traitors were good at what they did—they possessed either military might or political cunning. Adopting the enduring power of water was essential to keep these people from turning against the kingdom.

In 1643 the emperor of the Manchu Ch'ing dynasty (the last dynasty of China) passed away, leaving a six-year-old heir, Shun Zhi. At this time, the Ch'ing dynasty was in the midst of a decades-long war with the Ming dynasty. In order to ensure the position of her young son and the safety of the Ch'ing dynasty, the young emperor's mother, Xiao Zhuang, appointed his uncle Dua to perform all the emperor's duties until the boy was old enough to rule. It was said that as part of the price to ensure her son's position as future emperor, Xiao agreed to become Dua's mistress—a humiliation she endured for the sake of her son.

After the Ch'ing dynasty destroyed the Ming and General Dua also died, things looked better for Xiao. Or at least they did until her son, now the emperor, decided to leave the court to become a Buddhist monk. Her heart broken, Xiao stood strong and named her grandson, eight-year-old Kang Xi, emperor. This time she named four powerful elder generals as joint governing kings to perform the duty of emperor until her grandson could take over.

The most powerful governing king, O Bai, soon began "stealing" citizens' private land, taking bribes, and executing anyone who dared speak against him. The young emperor and Xiao knew about all this yet did not make a move to stop him because they did not yet have the power to eradicate him. They "ignored" their trusted officials' complaints and paid their normal respects toward General O Bai. Privately, Xiao told her angry young grandson, "Until you have the absolute power to destroy O Bai, do not make a move. If you do, he will eliminate you."

In 1667, fourteen-year-old Kang Xi finally took over the emperor's duties. At the age of sixteen, once he had built up enough power and support, he arrested General O Bai and his son and sentenced them to life imprisonment. Emperor Kang Xi governed China for sixty-one years and created the golden age of China. But without his grandmother's advice to tame the fire around him with the enduring power of water, he would have been burned by the powerful and greedy O Bai.

How does this apply to the workplace?

As I explained earlier, you cannot stop an attack. But you can fireproof yourself, to make sure you are not too badly hurt when the fire arrives. The alternative, as Sun Tzu reveals, is far worse:

> When a kingdom has been destroyed, it cannot come back into existence, just as a dead man can never rise.
>
> Thus a wise ruler heeds my warning, and the superior generals are cautious, because this is the way to keep a nation at peace and an army intact.

This is the exact principle Empress Xiao Zhuang followed. She made sure the young emperor did not make any foolish moves and kept the nation at peace by exercising the discipline of endurance. The same goes for you and I who work in today's complex business terrain.

Two Ways to Endure the Unendurable

The Chinese character for endurance is composed of two symbols: a knife sitting on top of a heart 忍. That is fitting, of course, because when you are forced to endure an unjust situation, it feels like a knife is cutting into your heart. Here are two strategies to help you endure those annoying people and circumstances that are holding you back.

1. Be patient. Recall the story of Vivian and Linda. If Vivian had chosen to stay at the bank, how could she have endured the fact that Linda had tarnished her reputation? With patience: by sticking it out, knowing that eventually people would recognize her integrity and see Linda for what she really was.

2. Transcend the experience of suffering. The word *endurance* implies you are suffering. Even if you can't stop the circumstances that are causing your suffering, you can transcend the experience.

How do you reach that state? By understanding that the people who harmed you acted out of ignorance or were motivated by stupidity. They thought they would gain something by hurting you. But you can rise above their actions through the force of your mental wisdom.

Imagine that your life is a basket, and the contents of that basket include both pleasant and unpleasant experiences and people. If your behavior is in line with Tao, righteousness, you will see the unpleasant situations as nothing but minor irritations that you have to dig through to get to the good stuff. In time, you may even be able to view these annoyances as lessons in disguise.

Winning with the Power of Water

To set fire to attack others, one must have the necessary
means in readiness. And there are favorable times and dates
to set fire.

Ironically, although Sun Tzu wrote a chapter about attacking by
fire, he never had all the favorable conditions in place to set fire
to his enemy. However, he did have the opportunity to use the
power of water; during an attack on the capital of Zhu, he redi-
rected the Zhang River to flood the city.

Women today need not use water in such a direct way; for
us, it makes much more sense to call on our natural ability of endurance. Success doesn't happen overnight—often it takes years
of dealing with bumps in the road as you wait for the right opportunity to present itself.

In short, change what you can, endure that which you cannot.

REFLECTION

Are you currently experiencing a trying situation at work—a difficult
colleague, a challenging project, an unglamorous title? Is it worth
enduring? What are the possible gains of enduring your current situation? What are the gains of doing something to change it?

_____

_____

_____

_____

_____

CHAPTER 13

Espionage

T hings really haven't changed in more than 2,500 years.

In Chapter 13 of his *Art of War,* Sun Tzu writes about the huge cost it takes to maintain an army and adds that *"for the lack of willingness to allocate the budget of [just a] hundred [pieces of] gold we do not know the condition of our enemy."*

According to Sun, anyone who refuses to spend the necessary amount of money to learn about his enemies is *"unqualified to command a large army, and is incapable"* of serving his king.

What's the best way to stay ahead of your competitors? By finding out all the information you can about their businesses. No matter what industry you work in, there are ways to spy on the competition without resorting to full-out industrial espionage. That is the subject of section 13.1

Of course, none of us wants to be the victim of espionage. That's why section 13.2 is devoted to ways you can protect yourself from con artists and those who wish to spy on you and your organization.

Espionage:
An Introduction

Thus there are five kinds of spies:

1. The village spy [a person who seems to share the same background with you]

2. An internal spy [a mole within the enemy's organization]

3. A counterspy [a double agent]

4. A doomed spy [a spy given false information and set up to be captured]

5. A survivor spy [one who is expected to survive and report back information gathered]

Once, after I gave a workshop for all the CEOs and CFOs in a specific industry, the conversation turned to a discussion of spying. One executive said something that I have always remembered: "Spying is something we all do, but no one wants to admit it."

No country can properly defend itself and survive without an effective network of spies. It's the same for corporations, many of which have more financial muscle than most small countries. These companies need aggressive offensive and defensive espionage structures.

Not all spying is as glamorous as it is portrayed in James Bond movies, with people breaking into locked offices in the dead of night, taking photos of secret plans with tiny cameras or planting listening devices.

In fact, much intelligence gathering simply comes from listening to what your competitors' employees say in everyday conversations. This is why Master Sun wrote that *"the knowledge of the enemy's disposition can be obtained only from other men."*

When you are poor, and research and development is costly, espionage becomes more attractive. Some Asian businesses have preferred to obtain technological advancements through cheap and effective covert means. They gained information in hours that took the competition decades and hundreds of millions or even billions of dollars to develop.

Bargain-Basement Espionage

Some of the less expensive ways to obtain proprietary business information follow. They don't call for you to buy blueprints from spies or stage dramatic break-ins in the middle of the night, but they can save you a lot of money and time.

1. Buy one piece and get the rest free. Reverse engineering is the means and reproduction is the aim. You simply buy an example of the product you are interested in making and then take it apart to determine how it was manufactured. Once you know how, you make the product yourself. No need to come up with original ideas; no research and development is required. Of course, keep in mind that there are laws prohibiting you from making facsimiles of patented products. Do your homework, then take what you can.

2. Inventive mooching. You can enter into a joint venture with another firm; it supplies the designs and you do the manufacturing. Once you truly understand how the designs are created and the intricacy of the product, you end the joint-venture arrangement and make the product on your own. Countless American companies that make everything from high-tech equipment to bicycles have been victimized by this kind of "inventive mooching." If you plan to outsource your manufacturing, think about what secrets you might be giving away in return for the cheaper labor.

3. Send in a mole. Not surprisingly, companies have learned to be wary of joint-venture partners and are reluctant to reveal key components. Such was the case of one American firm that subcontracted software development to a Japanese firm but encrypted the key algorithms to keep the Japanese firm from reproducing the chips themselves.

Undaunted, the Japanese company arranged to have one of its employees work inside the American firm, "to help bring our two companies closer together." As soon as the Japanese employee was accepted inside the American firm, he set out to find the unencrypted data. It did not take long.

You know the ending. The Japanese firm now owns the market for the product the American firm used to control.

4. Play the friendship card. Often you don't even have to try that hard to gain secret information, especially from American employees. Americans are famous for their openness with their friends. All you have to do is hang around with them long enough; they are bound to let a piece of secret information slip at a backyard barbecue or over a couple of beers.

5. Feign stupidity. Whenever I advise American companies that are doing business with Asians, I always insist that management tell their employees to say very little. This is difficult because most people like to show off and brag about how much they know.

As soon as one of their Asian partners asks a really elementary question, many Americans can't help but go on and on, until invariably they reveal something proprietary. Everyone except Americans seems to understand the importance of keeping secrets!

Once I was in China traveling in a jeep for ten hours with a group of Chinese executives with whom I was doing business. During the ride, they complained about the Japanese and their tight mouths.

"I asked one of them a very simple, textbook question," one of my traveling companions said, "but he refused to provide the answer. I knew the answer, of course, but I was just testing him. But he wouldn't answer."

Of course, the reason the man refused was probably because he knew he was being enticed into talking.

Attempting to gain valuable information simply by asking is common practice in Asia, but Americans are the only ones who answer every time they are asked. You can avoid giving away information simply by pretending that you do not know it.

6. *Get help from your friendly headhunter.* If you want to gain an industrial secret, you can always hire away the person who created it. This path frequently leads to litigation, but it is one that many companies follow nonetheless.

7. *Get to know those in the know.* In some industries—the movie business and book publishing come to mind—companies hire independent consultants to scout out talent and projects before they sign deals in their specific territories. Such scouts can be wonderful sources of information about what's going on in other areas of your industry or in industries that you need to know about. If you don't already have these kinds of "village spies" working for your organization, keep in mind that your competitor probably does.

Thinking About Protection

When exercising a military disposition, it is most important to conceal your intention, motives, and movements from your enemy; so that even the wisest spy will not be able to see through them.

195

American companies simply do not spend enough time thinking about how to protect their intellectual property. Ironically, because they don't think they can be the target of industrial espionage, they are.

13.2

Faces of Con Artists and Their Victims

> It is the potential Li [gain] that causes your opponents to come at you.
> It is the potential harm that you can cause your opponents that keeps them a distance away.

Though sometimes hard to spot, we've all met them: people who take our affection and love, then betray our kindness. They appeal to our good nature and use it against us. They don't just cheat us and take our money; they rock our faith in humanity.

Of course, I'm not advising you to become so cynical that you stop trusting people. You always want to have an open heart.

But you need to be on guard, especially when you start to see the signs of cunning and treachery in the people you deal with.

The Con Artist in the Cubicle

Every emperor in ancient China had a favorite eunuch who functioned as a confidant, gofer, psychologist, and shoulder to cry on. Many executives have the same sort of person in their employ. Maria, a senior vice president at a Fortune 500 firm based in Chicago, was one such executive. Her confidant was John, her personal assistant.

Unfortunately, Maria's confidant turned out to be nothing but a con man—albeit an incredibly charming one. As Maria put it later, "For someone with whom I was not having a romantic relationship, he certainly had a way of making sure I gave him my heart."

Not that he didn't give her reason to trust him—at first. There was the time that they were traveling on business and Maria discovered she needed a special battery for her camera. John went out in the middle of a snowstorm to get it.

He would go out of his way for Maria on a regular basis and (at first) want nothing in return. As they walked through a department store on their way back to a hotel on another business trip, John stopped to admire an Armani suit.

"I'll buy it for you," Maria said.

"Thank you, but no," John said. "I don't need it."

Maria was so impressed. Here, she thought, was a young man without greed. What she didn't recognize was that this was part of the con.

John started taking advantage of that trust in small ways. After about a year, he asked Maria if he could start working at home. "The commute is wasting about three hours a day. If I didn't have to do it, I could get more work done," he said.

Maria agreed. She bought John his own computer, fax, and printer, and paid to have separate telephone lines installed for him so that he could work from home.

About a year later, he said he wanted to move to Seattle to be closer to his family. Figuring that the technology would still allow him to get his work done, Maria agreed. She paid for all of the moving expenses. Not only did she agree to entirely new office equipment, she also agreed to John's request that she rent him a separate office "so I can be even more efficient."

Maria never saw the office, of course, and over time John began asking for more and more money for things—office supplies, new computers, and the like—that he never seemed to be able to find the receipts for.

It is not that Maria never suspected that John was conning

her, but she chose not to believe it. Until you find yourself in this kind of situation, you may not realize how difficult it can be to admit that someone's taking you for a ride. Every month John had some great story about how he couldn't find the phone bill, or the rental company lost the invoice, and every month Maria continued to write the checks for these (undocumented) expenses. And of course John was being paid a very handsome salary all the while.

Initially, Maria dismissed her concerns about the expenses by telling herself "at least his work remains exemplary," but that, too, began to change over time.

One of the "great" things about con artists is that if you ask if they can do something, they will always say yes, even if they have no intention of doing it.

John always sounded sincere when he said "Absolutely, no problem. You will have it tomorrow" whenever Maria asked him to do something.

But that began to happen less and less. Maria kept telling herself he couldn't be lying to her, not given how sincere he sounded and how well he had performed in the past. But over time he did less work and still received his paycheck.

It is interesting to note how John continued to be able to get away with all this. When he wasn't sincerely promising to do something that he had no intention of doing, he would skillfully muddy the waters. When Maria would ask about paperwork that would back up his claim that he spent several hundred dollars on a purchase, John would deftly raise an unrelated issue—"Did you hear that this or that company is thinking of expanding into China?"—to distract her attention. His hope—correct, as it turned out—was that Maria would soon forget about the missing paperwork.

To explain away the tasks he hadn't completed, John would say something like "Last night I worked so late, and I was so tired that I ended up deleting everything by mistake. When I tried to recover the file, I ended up damaging the hard drive. Now I have no hard drive at all. My life is ruined, just ruined."

Suddenly Maria had become the guilty party. She had pushed John so hard that she had ruined his life—and of course she had to give him several weeks to get everything back in order.

The Ultimate Crime

How did Maria finally catch him in the act? She asked John to send prototypes of a new product to opinion leaders for their evaluation and endorsement. Her hope was they would provide testimonials that the company could use in its ads. Instead of creating the necessary packages to send out, getting the right mailing addresses, and following up, John simply manufactured a couple of ringing endorsements from the opinion leaders. (To make sure that the responses seemed authentic, John created only a couple of endorsements; if he had actually sent out the packages, not everyone would have responded.)

Maria had no reason to suspect that the comments were false. It was only after she called one of the endorsers to thank him for his kind words that she learned the truth.

"I have never received any request from you nor did I give an endorsement," he said.

John was (finally) fired a short time later. How could Maria have been so oblivious? Clearly, she should have seen the pattern of behavior and fired John months before.

Why didn't she? Because almost all of us believe in human goodness. It takes us a long time to think that someone could deliberately set out to cheat us.

And while it's true that many people are good and honest, a con artist is always just around the corner to lend you a shoulder to lean or cry on. He or she will be there to hear all about your personal and professional problems. His charm will easily melt your heart, and her words will take away whatever doubts you have.

Compared with their sincerity and excessive kindness, the minor details of nonperformance and cheating on expense accounts will seem minor.

I have met many con men (and women) in my life. I think they are wasting their talents. They are extremely creative and have a flair for both drama and fiction. Who knows, if they actually put a little effort in, they could become bestselling authors or win an Oscar for best screenplay—or best actor!

The "Merits" of Con Artists

Con artists are reprehensible creatures. And yet . . . I have to admit that we could learn a thing or two from their intricate plots. Con artists are:

1. Creative in both designing their schemes and carrying out the cons.

2. Disciplined. They systematically work toward their objective.

3. Persistent. They never think about giving up.

4. Enthusiastic. They don't lie in bed and feel sorry for themselves. They are trying to get absolutely everything out of life that they can.

5. Positive. They don't doubt that their plan will work.

6. Opportunistic. They seize the moment.

7. Hard workers. They're always "on."

8. Cool under pressure. If you ask a con artist, "Are you conning me?" he or she will look you in the eye and say, "How could you think that after all we have been through together?"

9. Sympathetic. It is comforting to know that someone in the world "really understands you."

10. Empathetic. They'll seem to take on your problems as their own.

The Faces of Victims

The good news is, you can protect yourself by refusing to play the role of the victim. Here are some traits that con artists prey on.

1. Eternal optimism. Your eyes might be open, but you do not see anything negative—or potentially negative—in anyone.

2. Greed. You want to get something for nothing.

3. Insecurity. If you need people to butter you up and tell you how wonderful you are, a con artist will be happy to do so.

4. Neediness. You can always count on that sweet con artist to provide emotional comfort when no one else can. Of course, this will end up causing you even more pain in the future.

5. Power. The dark side of accomplishment is that it makes you a target. That's not to say you shouldn't strive for the top; when you get there, though, be careful.

6. Hunger for advancement. People may try to take advantage of your ambition.

Protect Yourself from Con Artists

While con artists are all around us, there are certain steps you can take to protect yourself.

1. Ponder your character flaws. The greatest antidote against someone setting you up to fail is to know your own character. If you are too trusting, recognize that you are vulnerable. If you expect something for nothing, know that you can expect people to try to exploit your greed.

2. Add a bit of logic to your gut feelings. We all know that we should trust our gut feelings. However, if we can find what is causing our gut to react the way it is, we will be far better off. If all you have is a gut feeling, it may be possible for a con artist to win your trust. But if you know why you feel the way you do, it is easier to remain resolute.

3. Don't be greedy. No one can con you if you want nothing from him or her.

4. Exhaust him or her. As we saw, one of the con artist's "best" traits is persistence. Let the con artist give you a song and dance and exhaust his or her entire bag of tricks, but don't give in. Eventually he or she will walk away.

5. Stay away. You can't be conned if you stay away from con artists.

Thinking About Con Artists and Their Victims

Although we would like to think otherwise, there *are* bad people in the world. And despite all our best efforts to protect ourselves, we still may get conned. Should it happen, let go of your hurt and move on. Consider it a lesson learned.

You may have just finished the last chapter, but this is not the end of the book. Because the chapters of *The Art of War* are interconnected, you can always go back to earlier chapters with the knowledge you gained from the later ones. Take, for example, the chapter on espionage. Before you launch such an attack, I suggest you examine how your plans fit into the basic elements of winning that you learned in the opening chapter. Is your proposed action consistent with Tao? Is the timing right? Only when your intentions are in line with these elements can you determine the proper course of action.

And just because you have closed this book does not mean your work is done. I encourage you to revisit the book whenever you face a difficult situation. Often, you'll discover that what at first glance seemed like a challenge is really the opportunity of a lifetime.

MY SPECIAL THANKS

The experience of writing this book was like conducting warfare. There were moments I was caught in the midst of the battle, when retreat was not an option, so I reached into myself and found new strength and inspiration to march forward. So, first, I acknowledge myself for being bigger than I thought I was.

This is my special thanks to the warriors who were intimately involved by my side during this warfare:

Sarah Rainone, my editor. She committed herself wholeheartedly to this book. Without her input, this book would not be the same. How lucky I am to have her.

Roger Scholl, Editorial Director of Currency, the commander in chief, who has effectively adopted *Sun Tzu's Art of War* during the entire process.

Anna Ghosh, my agent, who is a natural strategist. As Sun Tzu said, "She treated her soldiers [authors] as her children; and yet kept them on target, and never spoiled them."

I am indebted to a number of warriors at Doubleday, without whom this book would not have been possible: Talia Krohn for her thoughtful editorial suggestions; Kate Duffy and Ed

Crane for expertly keeping the book's schedule on track; and Terry Karydes and Gretchen Achilles for the book's beautiful design.

And it would be an unforgivable oversight not to thank the original author of *The Art of War* himself. I used as my primary source a copy of the earliest known version of Sun Tzu's Bing Fa known to man (and woman), which was written on bamboo strips and discovered in China's Silver Peacock Mountain in 1972. The tomb where the strips were found has been dated back to the early days of the Han Dynasty—around 206 B.C. I also used two books for reference: *Sun Tzu's Art of War*, translated by Lionel Geiles (Confucius Publishing, © 1977), and *Sun Tzu* (Wunan Group, © 1997). My editor also read two excellent English-language editions of *The Art of War* for background information: *The Art of War: The Essential Translation of the Classic Book of Life;* edited, translated, and with an introduction by John Minford (Penguin Classics, Deluxe Edition, © 2002 by John Minford) and *The Art of War,* translated by Thomas Cleary (Shambhala Dragon Editions, © 1988 by Thomas Cleary).